W9-DHG-237

The Tax Dilemma:

PRAYING for PEACE
PAYING for WAR

The Tax Dilemma:
PRAYING FOR PEACE, PAYING FOR WAR

Donald D. Kaufman

Introduction by John K. Stoner

Wipf & Stock
PUBLISHERS
Eugene, Oregon

"Kings" on page 12 is reprinted by permission of Doubleday & Co., Inc., from *Poems, Essays, and Letters* by Joyce Kilmer, copyright 1914, 1917, 1918, by George H. Doran Co.

Wipf and Stock Publishers
199 W 8th Ave, Suite 3
Eugene, OR 97401

The Tax Dilemma
Praying for Peace, Paying for War
By Kaufman, Donald D. and Stoner, John K.
Copyright©2006 Herald Press
ISBN: 1-59752-804-8
Publication date 6/28/2006
Previously published by Herald Press, 2006

TABLE OF CONTENTS

AUTHOR'S PREFACE

Until the middle of the twentieth century it was an appropriate and valid Christian witness to refuse bodily participation in war. But many have come to believe that the refusal of military service alone is no longer an adequate response to the military demons which threaten to destroy the people on Planet Earth. The nuclear age, coupled with the strategy of deterence, has made it possible for nations to play an extremely dangerous game of competitive survival. The arms race and military spending have escalated to unbelievable levels. The astronomical amounts of money being spent for "national defense" and the consequent theft from the poor of this world suggest that war taxes are too monumental an issue to be ignored. What if Jeanette Rankin, the first woman to serve in the United States Congress, is right? "All they that live by the sword shall perish by taxes."[1]

For twenty years or more there has been a renewed awareness of the ethical implications of paying Federal taxes. Yet, because the church is conservative in implementing its faith and because our preconditioning resists change no consensus on the issue has yet emerged. Through our voluntary or involuntary participation in war as taxpayers, we are party to injustice that staggers the mind.

Most persons who attempt to interpret the past also seek to understand the present and something of the future. Reflecting upon experiences of the past is often useful and certainly enlightening. If we are to have a usable past on the issue of taxes exploited for war purposes it seems necessary to gather these historical encounters into a readily accessible collection. *What Belongs to Caesar?* (Herald Press, 1969) was my first attempt to compile such information. More happenings have come to light in the years since its publication. These too may have instructive value to us who are looking for signs of God's guidance in our own time. Although the lessons of history are not easily learned, the likelihood of repeating the errors of the past is increased if we refuse to learn from our own and others' experiences. This booklet of true life happenings is offered to meet that need.

Senator George McGovern, making no pretensions about holding a pacifist position, once reminded members of the United States Senate that the administration will do well to heed the admonition of Edmund Burke, a distinguished legislator of an earlier day: "A conscientious man would be cautious how he dealt in blood." I firmly believe that war tax history has a special significance in understanding God's agenda in human history. Perhaps it is good to be challenged once again by the example of those who have tried faithfully to apply the gospel of Christ to complex and questionable tax requirements. According to Sören Kierkegaard, "The past which cannot become present is not worth remembering."

Finally, I owe a special word of appreciation to Jill Preheim Graber, James Klassen, Marilyn Klaus, Susan Wedel Krehbiel, Robert Kreider, Harold Regier, Paul M. Schrock, Perry Yoder, the members of my Koinonia group, and numerous other persons for their help in getting this book into print.

Another recruit in the Lamb's War,

Donald D. Kaufman

INTRODUCTION

"But what can I do? I am only one person." —Author Unknown

The most common response of people to the unprecedented moral crisis of the world arms race is a sense of futility. Many people will agree that the survival of the human race itself is in jeopardy. Few will agree as to what can be done about it. An even smaller number believe that they personally can do anything.

Moreover, it is distressing to observe how many people attempt to absolve themselves of any personal responsibility for the situation we are in. They blame the government, big business, fate, God, or the devil. There is a great deal of passing the buck.

Especially, of passing the buck to Caesar. In the form of taxes, that is. War taxes. Yes, the word is out: there is such a thing as taxes for war. The government, if it calls it anything, calls it defense spending. People with a commitment to speak the truth, such as Christians, have a responsibility to expose the deceptive euphemisms and call a war tax a war tax.

At which point we return to the words of our unknown author, and supply her with another quote: I can do something about the taxes I pay for war.

This book is about doing that something. Appendix D is itself worth the price of the book for the unusual brain waves which it creates. But there is much more.

The book issues a challenge to a wide audience—Christian and non-Christian. God's claim on humankind is universal. But I find the author probing the Christian conscience most directly. What does it mean for the church to be praying for peace and paying for war? Donald Kaufman explores this contradiction from many angles and draws on many sources, but all with a view to finding the path of Christian obedience.

I have heard many Christians say that they do not engage in war tax resistance or protest because it is ineffective. The government ultimately gets the money, the resister makes no impact, and the exercise is futile. Apart from the fact that this appeal for success is strange talk for people whose hero and leader ended up being crucified, I hear in this an unspoken message that also doesn't quite fit. The general demeanor of these folks toward society and government is one of studious conformity to accepted practice and one does not have to be richly endowed with imagination to infer that tax resistance or protest looks very risky to them. Which adds up to suggesting that their real reason for not engaging in tax resistance is that they think it would be too effective—in challenging accepted myths, clarifying the moral issue, and inviting the neighbor to take a similar stand.

In this regard, it might just be that the church should embrace tax resistance as the moral equivalent of disarmament. It has become fairly acceptable in at least some church circles to call on government to take risks for peace in the way of disarmament. In those circles it has not been unusual to look with some disdain on those who called for tax resistance as a form of response to the arms race. Given the meager successes of all the disarmament talks of history, including the 1978 United Nations Special Session on Disarmament, from a purely strategic point of view it might begin to occur to us that disarmament is such an intractable problem that we shall have to appeal to the people over the heads of the politicians to do something about it. But on a level deeper than calculating strategies for success, the church should be asking its members what is the *right* thing for them to do regardless of the consequences. If the generals, presidents, and ambassadors have decided to continue the arms race, shall the Christians continue to pay for it?

For the church (indeed, for any sizeable denomination of the church) to embrace war tax resistance as a spiritual commitment and a stated policy would be the moral equivalent of a government seriously embracing a policy of disarmament. Both would involve risk, both would be unprecedented, and both would be right.

But what government is ready to do the right thing on disarmament? And what church is ready to do the right on war taxes?

There are costs and risks involved.

John K. Stoner, Executive Secretary
Mennonite Central Committee Peace Section (US)
July 4, 1978

Kings

The kings of the earth are men of might,
And cities are burned for their delight,
And the skies rain death in the silent night,
    And the hills belch death all day!

But the King of Heaven, who made them all,
Is fair and gentle, and very small;
He lies in the straw, by the oxen's stall—
    Let them think of Him today!

—Joyce Kilmer

The Tax Dilemma:

PRAYING for PEACE
PAYING for WAR

No Dissenting Voice

There was a time when William James could say that "war taxes are the only ones men never hesitate to pay."[2] But no longer. Just as A. J. Muste once argued "that it is not really possible to separate conscription and war"[3] today it can be said that it is no longer possible to separate tax payments from war. Taxes and war are inextricably linked together. When governments wage wars, they eventually levy taxes on the citizens to pay for them. And Will Durant reports that "in the last 3,421 years of recorded history, only 268 have seen no war."[4] Furthermore, taxes which escalate to high levels during a time of war are seldom if ever reduced to the earlier level. As a result we are faced with permanent war and the perpetual danger of escalating military budgets. Higher appropriations than ever seem likely for the 1980s.

Death and Taxes Join Hands

Governments invariably claim the right to levy taxes. Benjamin Franklin understood this fact of life when he said: "Nothing is certain but death and taxes."[5] (More recently a *Punch* cartoon noted that "what the taxpayer resents is that they don't come in that order"! Another observed that "the difference between death and taxes is that death does not get worse every time congress meets.") Despite our claims of having freedom, most citizens of the United States live in bondage to death— the death created by war tax payments. Martin Luther King, Jr., observed that his own government was "the greatest purveyor of violence in the world today." That observation is substantiated by the fact that four to seven dollars of every ten collected in taxes in the United States go to pay for wars—past, present, and projected.

Drafted Dollars Come First

Preoccupied as some citizens are with paying too much tax, I suggest that the crucial issue has to do with the purpose for which tax monies are used, not the amount. Presently a large portion of the federal budget is going to the Pentagon. More and more money is budgeted annually for its support. While a young person can be exempted from personally serving in the armed forces, no one is easily exempted from making contributions to the military leviathan.

There are those who for centuries have carried out the mandate of Jesus not to kill fellow human beings, but to love them, even at the risk of being killed themselves. Their commitment to love and peace, however, has not always kept them from paying taxes for military purposes. Is there not a glaring contradiction here unless people are peacemakers in *both* body and property? Why should the Christian refuse service in the army if he does not refuse to pay taxes? Is there a valid moral distinction between performing military service and paying the taxes which make war possible?

> In the days when the state asked primarily for men to go to war, we were conscientious objectors. But now the primary tool of war is money. Can we still be conscientious objectors now?[6]

Each of us is called upon to answer that crucial question.

The Bible Says—Or Does It?

For most people it is out of the question even to think of tax refusal alternatives until they are convinced that the Scriptures either allow or support such action. Many

Christians feel that there is an indisputable biblical mandate to pay all taxes just as one pays for other financial obligations. Actually it may be more nearly correct to say that the New Testament teaches neither the payment nor the refusal of all taxes. Because of this it is most urgent that we reexamine our assumptions about what the Bible says on this subject.

If we recognize the limitations of being selective, it will be helpful to examine those references which are often used to justify unquestioning obedience to governmental demands (i.e., Mark 12:13-17 and parallel passages; Matthew 17:24-27; Romans 13:1-7; and 1 Peter 2:13-17). We dare not assume that a few verses can give us the total biblical understanding or the definitive Christian point of view on church/state relations. 1 Samuel 8:10-20, Jeremiah 43:10a, Daniel chapters 3—7, Acts 5:29, Ephesians 6:12, and Revelation 13 and 19, where the institution of government is viewed more critically, are not to be overlooked.

Unless we study each passage in the context of the historical situation and in the light of the total gospel, we will hardly understand the Bible properly in such matters. One of the biggest hurdles for Christians to overcome in considering the war tax issue is the widespread assumption that the Bible speaks with one voice regarding the necessity of tax payment to the governments. People try too hard to give an evenhanded recognition to the church and the state in our society.

One of the verses in the New Testament which has provided sanction for a myriad of wrongs is Jesus' reply to the Pharisees and Herodians concerning the tax paid to Caesar. "Render to Caesar the things that are Caesar's, and to God the things that are God's" (Mark

17

12:17). Many believe this directive legitimizes whatever government requires of us even though we should also protest its evil course on any issue.[7] However, the text may not be interpreted in such a way as to equalize God's and Caesar's rights. The total context suggests that Jesus was making a statement in which the second clause had considerable priority over the first. For Jesus the overarching loyalty was to God and it was this loyalty which determined the character of His loyalty to Caesar. Conflicting situations were resolved for Him by His primary relationship to God.

The "half-shekel tax" referred to in Matthew 17 is definitely the temple tax which each Jew over twenty paid for the operation of the sanctuary since the time of the Exodus. Although Jesus opposed the compulsory nature of the tax He definitely chose to support the Jewish pattern of worship. Following the destruction of the temple in AD 70, this tax was appropriated by Roman officials for Jupiter Capitolinus. We do know that Christians refused to pay taxes for Caesar's pagan temple in Rome. For this reason, we can understand how erroneous it is to deduce from this story about the temple tax a command for the payment of all taxes.[8]

Paul's letter to Roman Christians is carefully organized. The development of his letter suggests that chapters 12 and 13 bear a close relationship to each other and definitely belong together. Is it not significant that the author prefaces his discussion of "authorities" (13:1-7) with a long discussion on the practical implications of Christian love (12:1-21)? Several scholars are convinced that the writer expects Christians to discriminate between the demands of Caesar and the demands of God, giving to each only his due, "refusing to give to

Caesar what belongs to God."[9] To be subject to government allows for disobedience when God's command contradicts a government's requirements. God continues to have first claim on people's lives.

Similarly the segment concerning civil powers in 1 Peter 2:13-17 bears a striking resemblance to Romans 13. Peter encourages unconditional love to all men but not unconditional obedience or acquiescence to any government. The absolute and perfect subjection is to God and this servanthood gives no room for wickedness. It should be instructive to us that Peter and Paul, who recommended submission to the "authorities," both died as martyrs at the hands of "kings." This fact alone speaks volumes and serves as an eloquent testimony of how the Christians understood their role in relation to the state. As "citizens of heaven" they knew that their first obligation was to conduct their lives in a manner which would match their citizenship. During the sixteenth century, Anabaptists recovered this understanding when they declared that government is "outside the perfection of Christ".[10] In the face of testing by political authorities, their highest loyalty was to Christ. "It is a good thing to be law abiding," they said, "but it is better that we be Christ-abiding."[11]

While space here does not permit us to explore differing interpretations in depth, individuals and congregations are encouraged to research the resources[12] and to discuss the implications of Christian faith for tax realities. Open-minded listening and interaction is one excellent way in which congregations can become communities of discernment. As in ancient days there is a continuing need for people who have "understanding of the times, to know what Israel ought to do" (1 Chronicles 12:32).

19

The Bible, coupled with Spirit-directed concern, has plenty of guidance to offer. If we invite God to speak to us through it we will have joined in the quest of "doing the truth."

New Occasions Teach New Duties

In our technological age, new implications arise from conscientious objection to war. Despite the continuing need for personnel, the development of automated weapons makes it unnecessary to engage extensive manpower to carry on a war. Furthermore, sophisticated weapons have separated military personnel from visual or other physical contact with either an enemy or with civilian victims. William Stringfellow observes,

> This extraordinary change in warfare places military professionals and citizens back home in more nearly the same practical relationship to those who are being killed. And if it is tempting to suppose that remote proximity abolishes responsibility for the killing, it must be remembered that the use of apparently anonymous automated weapons exposes the common and equal culpability for slaughter of those who pull the trigger and those who press the button with those who manufacture the means and those who pay the taxes. . . .[13]

Sophisticated weapons are the primary tool of war and these require extraordinary amounts of money.

Although a person may not be drafted into the military, he is forced, in a real way, to support it with his tax money. Consequently, the conscription (or confiscation) of money has become more important than the conscription of people. Money and materials, not people, have become the essential ingredient for today's war.

Vast sums of money, secured through the Internal Revenue Service, are required to purchase and maintain the enormously expensive push-button weapons. Preparation for full-scale war in our day calls for "drafted dollars" rather than "drafted persons." The federal income tax is the chief link connecting each individual's daily labor with the tremendous buildup for war.

Paying for War While Praying for Peace

If we "see life clearly and see it whole" it seems artificial to distinguish between being a military warrior and paying government for the implements of war. Is it any wonder that people are agonized by the contradictions of paying for war while praying for peace? To insist on personally abstaining from war while paying for it with taxes suggests an ethical inconsistency. To finance and pay for an activity is to participate in it.

Most Christians simultaneously affirm the legitimacy of taxation by governments and the obligation we have to pay taxes for all purposes which do not conflict with the Christian conscience. How then can we obey God and not pay taxes? Unless, of course, we are involved in the shedding of blood.[14] And there's the rub.

Getting Away with Murder

If you were handed a gun, right now, and told to shoot a man—or drop napalm on a village—you couldn't do it. . . . But the same good people who would vomit at the sight of burning flesh and blood on our hands have no qualms paying taxes for somebody else to kill and burn.

If we are forced to face the issues, we make excuses. . . . The managers of the Empire will let us speak—as long as we hand over the young men and the cash. And we are afraid to refuse. . . .

21

The government could never get away with murder—in Vietnam or any place—without help. The War Machine must be fed warm bodies and cold cash by the millions.[15]

That is how John E. Steen of Santa Ana, California, saw the personal responsibility each citizen shared for involvement in the Vietnam war.

The issue seemed to be just as clear during the Revolutionary War period in America. In those days John Carmichael, a Scottish Presbyterian pastor in Chester County, Pennsylvania, had little sympathy with the nonresistant sects who refused to pay war taxes, but he saw no distinction between fighting and paying the cost of war. In his 1775 sermon on Romans 13 he asserted:

> . . . if it was unlawful and anti-Christian, or anti-scriptural to support war, it would be unlawful to pay taxes; if it is unlawful to go to war, it is unlawful to pay another to do it, or to go do it.[16]

Interestingly enough Carmichael's reasoning expressed accurately the perspective of Andrew Ziegler, another Pennsylvanian of that era, who believed that collecting taxes from his Mennonite people was equivalent to "forcing nonresistant people to go to war."[17] Apart from the danger involved in war, Ziegler could see "no difference between going to war and paying the tax by which the war was supported."[18]

In the first three centuries of their movement, Christians made a decisive witness against participation in warfare. Speaking on their behalf, Origen said: "We no longer wield the sword against a nation, and we no longer learn the art of war, for we have become sons of peace through Jesus our Leader. . . ."[19] It is questionable

22

whether the Christian witness against war in our time is clear because of the willingness with which we have financed Caesar's war. We need to remember that for years, even centuries, the church has blessed wars, consecreated Crusaders, baptized blitzes, and "passed the ammunition"—all this in taxes or through special appeals for material help. But the contradictions in this lifestyle have not gone unnoticed.

Questions People Ask

We have already alluded to some of the questions which arise whenever the issue of war taxes is brought into focus. Questions are both necessary and helpful in finding answers to perplexing ethical problems. Do you find any of your questions among the following?

Is it patriotic to pay war taxes?

Are there biblical or Christian reasons for not paying taxes?

Do persons who knowingly and willingly pay taxes that support war claim to be innocent of the death and destruction that militarism inflicts upon other people?

Can a Christian in our day pay war taxes and still consider himself to be a bonafide conscientious objector to war?

Are Christians being too compliant when they obey every government demand?

Are Christians correct in challenging the right of a government to tax them for waging war?

What is the annual financial contribution which each family in North America makes toward war through taxation?

Is concern about war taxes a new issue, or is there a history of tax refusal?

Should every person, on receipt of the government's demand for money to kill, hurry as fast as he can to comply?

Should Christians take their obligations toward government more seriously than their church obligations?

Unless people dissent from paying war taxes, how are government leaders to know that Christians are opposed to making war on other peoples called "enemies"?

How can people reduce their complicity in war under present IRS regulations?

Are there people who have risked obeying God rather than the IRS?

Is there a difference between what God expects of us as individuals compared to what He expects of us when we participate in groups?

Why are church institutions so timid in the face of evil?

Does God expect us to follow the dualistic "two-kingdom ethic" with governmental demands taking precedence over our personal moral obligations?

Do we really have moral responsibility for the tax money we pay once it is in the government's treasury?

Are we accountable to both God and Caesar in equal measure?

Is there a necessary incompatibility between Christian love and paying taxes?

If participation in warfare makes me guilty of sin and if I pay taxes to the Government for military purposes, do I not share moral responsibility for the killing which the Government does in my name?

Does the proportion of government monies used for military purposes have any bearing on the Christian's general obligation to pay taxes?

If accountability is related to control and the ability to affect decisions, is it proper to hold people accountable for evil consequences over which they appear to have little or no control?

Is there clear bibical teaching that all taxes levied by government should be paid without resistance?

Do you see the conscientious objection to paying war taxes as a logical extension of being a conscientious objector to war?

Is there really no difference between performing military service and paying war-related taxes?

Would you support legislation which would enable citizens to designate a percentage of their income tax (equal to the military portion of the federal budget) to a world peace fund?

Should a church agency withhold taxes from its employees as required by law, even if more than fifty percent of the tax goes for military purposes?

Could a government ever be so unjust and murderous in its policies that you would resist paying taxes to it?

How much responsibility can the rulers assume over our consciences, and how much obedience can they rightfully demand?

Can we really accept paying taxes to support "a hospital that butchers two and heals one?"

How can we maintain our integrity as persons while giving to such diametrically opposed causes?

What constitutes faithfulness for a congregation wanting to take a position on war tax payment?

Can the Scriptures provide us with the means of testing whether or not payment of war taxes constitutes a form of idolatry?

Must we personally survive at the expense of others in our world who are less powerful?

"Suppose Caesar would level a 10 percent tax to pay for the extermination of Mennonites. Would we encourage everyone to 'render unto Caesar what he asks for'?"[20]

In God's eyes does it make a difference whose death a government asks us to pay for?

Everybody's Doing It

Human beings are often inclined to make excuses. As one maxim puts it, "Whenever you need an excuse, any excuse will do." There is good precedent for paying taxes. Furthermore, the penalties imposed for not paying taxes help to keep us sufficiently motivated. But what if we comply for the wrong reason? Are public pressures and expectations necessarily the voice of God? Are the majority decisions of elected governments infallible decisions about good and evil? Specifically, is it right for me to pay war taxes just because others are doing it?

M. Kamel Hussein focuses on such a dilemma in his dramatic interpretation of the life of Jesus, *City of Wrong: A Friday in Jerusalem*. The core theme of his book examines "the collective as man's all too frequent plea to justify wrong."[21] Somehow the greatest crimes are easily perpetrated when responsibility for those acts is distributed among many persons. A small share of the blame is hardly significant enough for the conscience to bother about. When everyone is responsible no one is responsible. Hussein contends that the crucifixon of Jesus, an obvious wrong, "was carried through by dint of being parceled out among a large number of people so that no single individual had any longer to think of himself as personally responsible."[22] But communal consent is no guarantee of innocence. Here is the reason why:

> Men in communities take differing attitudes from those of individuals towards right and wrong and whether to act or not to act. Communities readily do the wrong because the individuals composing them share out the weight of guilt and none of them feels personally implicated. Each thinks of his partners as exempting him from implication in that his particular share of responsibility is very slight. He argues too that even if he had not participated it would have happened anyhow. Communities as such are not readily inclined to take action for the good, because the individuals who make them up prefer to have the credit. When, however, communities abstain from their obligations toward what is good that does not absolve individuals from reproach and pangs of conscience. For then each individual feels himself culpable, not having performed his proper duty, even though he is not alone in his disinclination and his reluctance for risks.[23]

This excerpt identifies sin as "collective irresponsibility." Sin seems to disappear whenever a group of people can be made to share the responsibility for what would be a sin if an individual did it. The load of guilt rapidly lifts from the shoulders of persons when the guilt is shared. The lynching of blacks, the mass murder of Indians and Japanese by the United States, and the Nazi attempt to liquidate the Jews all serve as examples of group violence where the indivudal is less and less clearly accountable for his actions or those of his group.

Karl Menninger points out that—

No one disputes the evilness of the dreadful acts of war, but who is guilty? Not I, I obeyed orders. Not I, I merely

27

transmitted the orders. Not I, I issued the orders on the basis of command decisions. Not I, I was only the executive of the managerial group. Not we, we specified a general objective in keeping with the national purpose.[24]

Is this the kind of sanction which makes it possible for us who are conscientiously opposed to war to keep on paying the taxes which make it possible? How can we be freed from blind obedience to those demonic powers which make Auschwitz's ovens a mere prelude to the brutality of man?

Waves of War Tax Concern

War tax anxiety, long buried in history, is coming to life again. Looking at 460 years of Anabaptist history it appears that there were three major waves of concern: (1) among the Hutterites of the sixteenth century who courageously put word and deed together at great risk to their own lives; (2) among the Brethren, Quakers, Mennonites, Moravians, and Schwenkfelders of Colonial America who despite the risks of disloyalty were committed not to offend God or their consciences; and (3) among people of North America who, out of the agony of war during the past two decades, have come to recognize the inconsistency of praying for peace while paying for war.

War has a way of bringing out the best as well as the worst in human beings. Because it is a crisis experience for the people involved, such situations have created opportunities for growth in following Jesus. They have also revealed the shallowness of much Christian commitment. Fortunately the vision is not limited to those who call themselves Christian. The following items help put the "taxes for war" issue in historical perspective.[25]

Blood Money and Protection Refused

The Hutterites of the sixteenth century took a strong position against what they termed "blood money." They consistently refused to pay war taxes and special levies. In 1545 Peter Riedemann wrote:

> For war, killing, and bloodshed (where it is demanded especially for that) we give nothing, but not out of wickedness or artibrariness, but out of the fear of God (1 Timothy 5) that we may not be partakers in strange sins.[26]

Claus Felbinger, another Hutterite brother, confirmed this perspective in a written confession of 1560:

> Therefore we are gladly and willingly subject to the government for the Lord's sake, and in all just matters we will in no way oppose it. When, however, the government requires of us what is contrary to our faith and conscience—as swearing oaths and paying hangman's dues or taxes for war— then we do not obey its command. This we do not out of obstinancy or pride, but only out of pure fear of God. For it is our duty to obey God rather than men (Acts 5:29).[27]

Felbinger and a partner were beheaded on July 19, 1560. Their witness was clear and unequivocal. Despite intense pressure and considerable hardship, the Hutterite witness continued well into the nineteenth and twentieth centuries. Some Anabaptists did not have as strong a position on this issue. There was disagreement among several groups in Europe.

One of the clearest and most appropriate instances of war tax refusal in North America took place in 1637 when the relatively peaceable Algonquin Indians opposed taxation for armaments by the Dutch. After having sold arms to the Iroquis Indians, William Kieft tried to pacify the offended Algonquins by improving Fort Amsterdam which he claimed was to provide protection for Algonquins as well as for the Dutch settlers. When he sent his tax collectors to the Indians they were met with a storm of resistance: "Protection indeed! His fort was no protection to them. They had not asked to build it, and were not going to help maintain it."[28]

A Potent Witness for Peace

The American Quakers made refusal of war taxes an integral part of what was undoubtedly one of the most potent witnesses for peace and against war in any age by any people. As early as 1711 William Penn informed the Queen of England that his conscience would not allow "a tribute to carry on any war, nor ought true Christians to pay it."[29] Then in 1715 an anonymous Quaker argued with even greater certainty in a pamphlet entitled *Tribute to Caesar*.

> To pay ordinary taxes is justifiable, of course, and it is not always necessary to inquire what the government does with them. But when taxes are levied specifically for war purposes, and announced as such, the Christian must refuse to pay them, says the author. Hence the expedient of voting money "for the queen's use" in response to a demand for military aid is a sacrifice of principle.[30]

Tax refusal as a moral protest against war was already practiced by the Quaker assembly of the Colony of Pennsylvania in 1709. They refused to grant the £4,000 which was requested by the English Crown for an expedition into Canada, but voted to give £500 to the queen as a token of respect, provided that "the money should be put into a safe hand till they were satisfied from England it would not be employed in use of war. . . ."[31]

John Woolman (1720-72) admitted that he had longstanding scruples against paying taxes "for carrying on wars." He could see no effective difference between actually fighting a war and supporting it with taxes. In his *Journal,* he wrote:

> To refuse the active payment of a tax which our society generally paid was exceeding disagreeable, but to do a thing contrary to my conscience appeared yet more dreadful. . . . Thus, by small degrees, we might approach so near to fighting that the distinction would be little else but the name of a peaceable people.[32]

The tax resistance movement was given good footing in 1755 when Dunkards (Church of the Brethren) and Quakers refused to pay taxes for the French and Indian campaigns of the Seven Years' War.[33] During that military conflict, the Quakers—John Woolman, Anthony Benezet, and John Churchman—led a protest movement against passage of a tax bill that included provisions for killing Indians. After the "militia bill" was passed (November, 1755), they refused to pay their taxes "though suffering be the consequence of refusal." Twenty-one years later, one of the tests of a Quaker's sincerity was his refusal to pay taxes for the Revolutionary War.[34]

All Civic Obligations—Save One

The nonresistant sects fulfilled all civic obligations— save one. They were not willing to participate in war either bodily or through financial contributions. They claimed indulgence on no other point. One patriot lamented the lack of cooperation received from the Dunkards:

31

> They refused in the most positive manner to pay a dollar to support those who were willing to take up arms to defend their homes and their firesides . . . they were *non-resistants!* They might, at least, have furnished money, for they always had an abundance of that, the hoarding of which seemed to be the sole aim and object of life with them. But, no; not a dollar![35]

Unfortunately when money was given, the authorities understood their voluntary contributions "for the needy" as donations to the war chest. It did not matter where Quakers, Mennonites, or Brethren lived, the problem of paying for war soon caught up with them. Not infrequently questions arose from the war on which they could not all agree. The expulsion of Bishop Christian Funk in 1777 was a result of this debate over the propriety of paying Congressional war taxes.[36] Funk had taken the position in favor of payment.

On November 7, 1775, Mennonites and Church of the Brethren people submitted a joint declaration to the General Assembly of the Commonwealth of Pennsylvania. In that petition the Dunkards and Mennonites said they were ready at all times to help those in need or distress—

> —it being our Principle to feed the Hungry and give the Thirsty Drink;—we have dedicated ourselves to serve all Men in every Thing that can be helpful to the Preservation of Men's lives; but we find no Freedom in giving, or doing, or assisting in any Thing by which Men's Lives are destroyed or hurt.[37]

The Faithful Church in a Hostile World

In Prussia both military and church taxes were based on land ownership. Mennonites were disinclined to pay for the support of either the military or the state church. By the 1780s they were apprehensive about the growing military preparations, particularly the annual tax of 5,000 thaler required for the support of military schools. This factor prompted many to relocate in southern Russia.[38]

Klass Reimer, a Mennonite minister of Danzig and later of Molotschna in Russia (1805 f.), "was opposed to contributions made to the Russian government during the Napoleonic War."[39] He was appalled at the lack of personal morality and ethical concern among the Mennonites. To promote his concern for the restoration of an authentic biblical-Anabaptist Christianity, he began meeting with like-minded Christians in 1812, and by 1814 they were organized as a separate group (the "Kleine Gemeinde").

Caught Between Two Fires

Perhaps one of the severest tests to which peace principles were ever put occurred in Ireland during the rebellion of 1798. During that terrible conflict, the Irish Quakers were continually caught between two fires. The Protestant faction viewed them with suspicion because they refused to fight or to pay military taxes, and the insurgents thought they should be killed because they would neither profess belief in the Catholic religion nor help them fight for Irish freedom.[40]

Difficult as it was to meet public hostility, Quakers and the Brethren did not hesitate to exercise discipline on those who failed to follow the historic peace teaching of the church. By and large Mennonite opposition to war taxes was not as intense as that of the Quakers. What agonizing predicaments the conscientious objectors found themselves in, for they were punished by the state if they did not support war efforts and by the church if they did!

The Shakers in New Hampshire, a people that tried to remake society, were not as ambivalent as Mennonites about their response to the demands of war. In 1818 they addressed the Legislature in the following terms:

> Anything then of the coercive nature, under whatever name, practised against conscience, must be a pointed violation of these rights. . . .
>
> And should we consent to pay a tax as an equivalent this would be a virtual acknowledgement that the liberty of conscience is not our natural right; but may be purchased at a stated price.
>
> Such a concession involves in it, a principle derogatory to the Almighty, because it requires us to purchase of government, liberty to serve God with our persons, at the expense of sinning against him with our property.
>
> . . . we feel ourselves impelled by the most sacred obligations of duty, to decline . . . let the consequences be what they may.[41]

An Influential Night in Prison

The United States war against Mexico in 1846 is important to our review because it and the Massachusetts poll tax provoked Henry David Thoreau to write his famous essay on civil disobedience.[42] Thoreau's essay is a justification for opposing the state when law and conscience conflict. He tried to give encouragement to timid persons who held social justice concerns but who did not dare to say "no"—did not dare to disobey the government that perpetuated evils which they deplored. Because Thoreau viewed slavery as an unmitigated evil he rejected the war and refused to pay the tax levied to support it. Rejecting the assumption that the citizen must support all governmental activities, even those which fall short of being just, he asserted that government "can have no pure right over my person and property but what I concede to it." Consequently he decided for himself that certain taxes were morally justified and that certain others were not. For him the refusal to pay taxes was an effort to use his "whole influence" to stop "a violent and bloody measure." There will never be a really free state, he said, "until the state comes to recognize the individual as a higher and independent power, from which all its own power and authority are derived, and treats him accordingly." Furthermore it was his conviction that "if in a country the government acts wrongly, then a prison is the only place a self-respecting citizen can live in."[43] Considering his impact upon millions of people through Tolstoy, Gandhi, and Martin Luther King, Jr., his individual witness was obviously profound.

Leo Tolstoy (1828-1910), deeply impressed by the Sermon on the Mount, understood conscientious objection to war to include the problem of war taxes.

> "You may wish to make me a participator in murder; you demand of me money for the preparation of weapons; and want me to take part in the organized assembly of murderers;" says the reasonable man—he who has neither sold nor obscured his conscience. "But I profess that law— the same that is also professed by you—which long ago forbade not murder only, but all hostility also, and therefore I cannot obey you."[44]

Your Money or Your Life!

By the time of the Civil War, the Quakers were still vigorously protesting war taxes, but the Brethren and the

Mennonites were more inclined to pay whatever the government required of them. Of course, there were individual protests such as the one made by a Quaker named Maule who became concerned over the lax spiritual condition of many of his friends who were not disturbed by taxes levied for war purposes. He refused to pay the County Treasurer 8½ percent of the tax for 1861, "which was the part expressly named in the tax list as for the war at that time."[45]

During the American Civil War both systems of national conscription offered two alternatives to pacifists. Exemption from the draft could be obtained either by furnishing an acceptable substitute or by paying $300 ($500 in the South) for hiring one. There was considerable opposition to this arrangement among the conscientious objectors because the only way of securing exemption was to hire a substitute, either directly or indirectly. And it did not seem consistent to hire another person to do that which one could not conscientiously do oneself.[46]

"To Pay an Onerous Tax"

At the time that Mennonites were migrating to Kansas an existing law (1865) required the payment of a thirty-dollar fine payable each May for the privilege of exemption from military service. Apparently Governor Osborne saw this as an infringement on the citizen's freedom and as a disadvantage in securing Mennonite immigrants for Kansas. On January 15, 1874, he proposed an amendment to the existing law. The governor said:

It is hoped that large accessions may be made of these worthy settlers, and it may properly be considered whether any class of people who are conscientiously opposed to bear-

36

ing arms should be compelled to pay an onerous tax to be relieved therefrom. It strikes me as incongruous that such religious convictions should be taxable by our laws.[47]

In response to the governor's recommendations, the legislature repealed the "onerous tax" on March 9, 1874.

"Justified in Giving Neither Money nor Soldiers"

The Vyborg Manifesto of July 23, 1906, gave the people of Russia new freedom. Having dissolved the government it declared that the populace was "justified in giving neither money nor soldiers."[48] Years later the triumph of the Bolsheviks in October of 1917 produced a reign of terror for the Mennonites. Despite attempts to remain nonresistant and loving the struggle for survival resulted in desperate measures. Mennonite young people yielded to the spirit of militarism and organized the Self-Defense Corps. This proved to be not only a tactical blunder but also a gross violation of historic biblical faith.[49] In this episode some Mennonites obviously financed war preparations. Among the Dutch Mennonites practically all opposition to war was gone by 1900. Having become respectable and wealthy in their society they suffered a loss of vitality and a serious decline in membership (200,000 to 30,000). It is reported that "they won the good will of the state on several occasions by making very substantial contributions in money when their country was at war."[50]

World War I—A Watershed Experience

For Mennonites, World War I was a severe test of their Christian faith. As their most profound civic identity crisis in America, it proved to be a turning point in their history. According to James C. Juhnke, a Mennonite historian, the leading issues in the confrontation between the nonresistant Mennonites and the crusading Americans were "military service, the war bond drives, and the German language." They cooperated with patriotic expectations as best they could, "developing their own programs of voluntary benevolence and relief to provide a moral equivalent of military service and war bond drives."[51] At the beginning it was generally agreed among the Mennonite leadership that participation in the war effort through the purchasing of bonds was wrong. But with increased pressure practically everyone "bought a few bonds." Bond drives were designed not only to finance the war but also to foster patriotism. Margaret Entz described the results of this in Kansas as follows:

Refusal to buy war bonds was one of the standards by which the American patriotic community judged the Mennonites to be unworthy of their citizenship. Bonds were not only of monetary value, they also symbolized patriotic support of American's war effort along with her ideals of democracy and liberty. By attaching these values to the Liberty Loans, the Treasury Department succeeded remarkably in selling bonds. In light of the fact that the war economy was not a matter of consumer choice and was imposed upon people involuntarily, this achievement was even more notable. Necessary war financing was done through voluntary means in order to gain the support of the American people, but with demanding methods that necessitated compliance from all.

Mennonites were caught in this contradictory government policy. If bonds were truly voluntary, then purchasing them was an intentional contribution to a cause the Mennonites abhorred. However, the Treasury Department undermined the principle of voluntarism by urging the necessity of bond purchases on the local level. Mennonites were scorned, intimidated, threatened, and physically harmed until they bought bonds. The war that failed miserably to make the world safe for democracy, also failed to perpetuate democracy at home.[52]

To Pay or Not to Pay, That Is the Question

To illustrate the consequences of the government's World War I strategy we mention three peacemaking incidents from that period.

John Schrag, a farmer from rural Burrton, Kansas, became the victim of mob violence on November 11, 1918, when he was forced to buy war bonds or bear the consequences. He was beaten, smeared with yellow paint, imprisoned, and taken to court for disrespect to the American flag. Despite the unforgettable jolt, he could not support the war and hate Germany. Years later, Charles Gordon, a member of that mob testified to Schrag's calmness throughout the ordeal: "He exemplified the life of Christ more than any man I ever saw in my life."[53]

Another encounter with zealous patriots took place near Bloomfield, Montana, where Pastor John Franz and members of the Bethlehem congregation were criticized for their refusal to take part in the war. Specifically, they were asked why they refused to buy war bonds. In responding to this challenge Pastor Franz tried to explain that—

Christians really own nothing. We are here to take care of all God's things. Since our money is God's money, we can use it only for things that please Him. We cannot buy war bonds, because that makes war possible. Using our money

39

to make it possible for others to be killed would be just as wrong as going into the army and killing a man ourselves.[54]

Several years later one of the twelve men who had tried to hang Pastor Franz stopped to ask him a sober question: "Will you forgive me for the great wrong I did to you and to your family?"

In keeping with their belief in the necessity of civil government, Hutterites pay all taxes levied against them except war taxes. The latter are refused in obedience to the lordship of Christ.[55] Although willing to contribute money for the relief of war sufferers, the Hutterites in South Dakota refused to purchase Liberty Bonds. Most also refused to contribute to the Red Cross.

> When a local bond committee assigned the Hutterites a quota, and they refused to buy any bonds, a group of patriotic enthusiasts visited the Jamesville colony and without opposition drove away a hundred steers and a thousand sheep. They were shipped to the livestock market, the proceeds to be invested in war bonds. The packing houses, however, refused to take the stolen cattle, and they had to be sold at auction in Yankton for about half of their value.[55]

All three of the above accounts remind us of the need for creative imagination in applying the gospel, courage to endure persecution and suffering, and deep commitment to implement faithfully the way of the cross. A moving hymn suggests the nature of the conflict:

> Once to every man and nation comes the moment to decide,
> In the strife of Truth with Falsehood, for the good or evil side. . . .
> New occasions teach new duties, Time makes ancient good uncouth;

They must upward still, and onward, who would keep
abreast of Truth. . . .
Though the cause of evil prosper, yet 'tis truth alone is
strong.
Though her portion be the scaffold, and upon the throne be
wrong,
Yet that scaffold sways the future, and, behind the dim
unknown
Standeth God within the shadow keeping watch above His
own.[56]

Strong Decisions, Careful Citizens

The "Merchants of Death" debate raged through the
1930s. In 1933 a query on protesting against military
taxes was brought to the annual Church of the Brethren
Conference. It was answered the following year by a
report from the Board of Christian Education which
listed several methods of protest but not including the
refusal of payment.[57] Apparently this possibility did not
enter the minds either of those bringing the query, the
Board that formulated the answer, or the conference that
adopted it. With the exception of the 1781 minute that
allows tax refusal as a conscientious possibility, it was not
until 1968, the peak of the Vietnam War, that any of the
church's many statements on war as much as took note of
the matter. In that year the revision of the original 1948
statement on war added a significant section on "The
Church and Taxes for War Purposes."

For the most part the war tax issue remained dormant
during World War II. Among the first of the Mennonites
to mention the subject was a nonregistrant, Austin
Regier, who was sentenced to one year and one day in
federal penitentiary for refusing to comply with the
draft. Firmly committed to the way of love and indi-

41

vidual responsibility, he believed that "the consistent pacifist should refuse war taxes."[58]

Peace Agitator

A. J. Muste (1875-1967) was regarded by many as the outstanding spokesman in the United States for the Christian pacifist position. As early as 1936 it was his conviction that the most effective thing which people in the world could do was "to dissociate themselves completely from war." Muste worked energetically with the war tax problem, refusing from 1948 on to pay Federal income taxes. Not until 1951 was he questioned by Internal Revenue agents, and not until 1960 was he brought into court. Whenever there was opportunity he articulated the position that there should be alternatives to making H-bombs or paying for making them. He repeatedly challenged the right of the government to tax him for waging war. From his perspective,

> . . . the two decisive powers of government with respect to war are the power to conscript and the power to tax. In regard to the second I have come to the conviction that I am at least in conscience bound to challenge the right of the government to tax me for waging war, and in particular for the production of atomic and bacterial weapons.[59]

The Peacemaker Movement

The idea of organizing war tax resistance in this country seems to have begun with the Peacemaker Movement which was formed by 250 pacifists in Chicago early in 1948. This heterogenous group of Americans are united by their refusal to pay taxes so long as the federal budget is weighted so heavily by military expenditures. Since coming together they have been saying "no" to

42

conscription for war and making the alternatives known to others through their publication, *The Peacemaker*. Since February 1963, the Movement has also published a useful *Handbook on Nonpayment of War Taxes* which contains alternative suggestions and numerous personal histories.[60]

An update on the Peacemaker witness is pertinent. In 1975 the Internal Revenue Service discovered itself in a "no win" position and subsequently returned to Gano Peacemakers, Inc., the house near Cincinnati which had been seized by the IRS earlier. This experience confirmed for Ernest and Marion Bromley, former editors of *The Peacemaker*, the knowledge that the authorities of death are *not* all-powerful. For the Bromleys there is no reason to fear the IRS. Mrs. Bromley reported:

> One of the pleasant feelings we have about the reversal of the sale (besides knowing that we can continue to live on these two acres) is that many people have told us they got a real lift when they heard that some "little people" had prevailed in the struggle with the IRS. We had the feeling that our daily leafleting and constant public statements during the seven months' campaign had, at least, the effect of showing that people need not *fear* this government agency. People do fear the IRS and that is an unworthy attitude. What can they take away that is of real value?[61]

Confronting Congress and the IRS

One of the leading peace movements of the past fifty years is the War Resisters League. Since its inception in 1923, the League has sought to create a just and peaceful society through nonviolet and life-supporting methods. Jessie Wallace Hughan, one of WRL's founders, articulated its first policy on war taxes in a 1935 pamphlet. Al-

43

though she didn't advocate resistance at that time, she urged taxpayers to consider "taxation as a form of seizure, not a voluntary contribution." War tax refusal has been an ongoing activity of the League since the 1940s. By 1953 demonstrations at IRS Centers were being held. The first WRL call for total tax resistance was issued in 1957. Marion Bromley, a League member and one of the founders of Peacemakers, wrote:

War resisters pledge they "will not support any kind of war." If we have reached the point where the major "support" that is demanded is financial, is it not time to break ranks, to bring the deed more nearly into harmony with the pledge?[62]

From that point on, the League considered tax resistance a basic, if not central, part of its program. One of the movement's most joyous occasions took place in 1969 when resisters formed War Tax Resistance, a new and distinct organization whose activities would focus solely on all aspects of tax refusal. Working with vigor and imagination the movement has moved into new forms of resistance activity such as court appeals for employee rights against the withholding of war taxes. The League's confrontation with the Internal Revenue Service in 1974 resulted in the seizure by IRS of $3,432.58 from its bank account. This experience confirmed the need for a continuing protest despite the hassles and the risks. *Liberation* magazine, begun in 1956, and *Win,* begun in 1965, are two effective instruments for propagating nonviolent insights and the astounding costs of militarism.

Similar to the WRL is the Central Committee for Conscientious Objectors which began in Philadelphia in

44

mid-1948 to deal with conscription issues. By 1956, realizing that conscientious objection relates not only to the draft but to all conflicts between the state and moral choice, CCCO extended its services to objectors to include tax payments for war purposes. The Milton Mayer Defense Fund to reclaim war taxes was one of their primary accomplishments during the 1950s. In the 1960s a number of staff members were tax resisters. CCCO policy has always been to refuse to honor IRS levies so as not to become a collection agency for the IRS. In 1978 for the first time, IRS has brought suit against CCCO for their failure to pay the tax debt allegedly owed by a past employee who has refused for reasons of conscience. Steven Gulick bases his position on the Quaker teaching that one should not support war or preparations for war.[63]

Would Jesus Pay for Atom Bombs?

Two of the key figures in the anti-war tax movement have been deeply concerned about the poor in our society. They are Ammon Hennacy (1893-1970) and Dorothy Day (1897-   ). Both of these forceful leaders have been actively involved in the Hospitality Houses operated by the Catholic Worker Movement. Catholic opposition to war has taken on new significance since the founding of the movement in 1933. In January of 1942, Dorothy Day wrote to her fellow workers:

> We are still pacifists. Our manifesto is the Sermon on the Mount, which means that we will try to be peacemakers. . . . We will not participate in armed warfare or in making munitions, or by buying government bonds to prosecute the war, or in urging others to these efforts.[64]

More recently she declared:

Working for a better order here in this world means a terrible struggle. . . . Our means are prayer and fasting, and the nonpayment of federal income tax which goes to war.[65]

Bernard Survil of Indianapolis, Indiana, has been part of a group called Ammon's Tax Associates since the early 1970s. As a Roman Catholic priest he has brought together a group of concerned persons who are committed to the study and practice of war tax objection. They urge churches to help legitimize war tax objection as a moral alternative to war. In 1971 they submitted a 7-page "Plea for Support" to the American Bishop representatives to the Roman Synod. Ammon's Tax Associates sense that an individual may make a conscientious decision to withhold war taxes when three elements concur:

(1) He has enough specific information which he accepts as true with a sufficiently high degree of confidence.

(2) He experiences the moral imperative to act upon this information in this individual way, after weighing the matters of moral integrity, the usefulness or effectiveness of the act in accomplishing its purposes, as well as considering the accompanying effects not willed directly but which will most likely follow from the decision.

(3) The courage (or foolhardiness) to go through with it.[66]

The reason war tax objection is so rare is that few people can honestly say that they feel informed enough to move beyond step 1. Many persons could be moved from indecision to action by increasing their awareness of the issue and its implications.

A Call to Action Conference held in Detroit recommended that the Catholic Church—

> . . . give its support to those who on grounds of conscience refuse to serve in war or preparation for war; that Catholics support legal provision for selective and general conscientious objection to military service and to the payment of war or military taxes.[67]

Among the more militant leaders of the Catholic war resistance movement are Daniel and Philip Berrigan, David Miller, and Tom Cornell, all of whom have been convicted in federal courts for acts growing out of their religious objection to the war system.

During the past two decades, Brethren, Quakers, Mennonites, and others have become increasingly disturbed over the large portion of tax monies which contribute so heavily to finance past, present, and future wars. It has been calculated that out of a 12-month tax period the United States taxpayer works nearly six months before his federal income tax has paid for anything beyond current military expenses and the cost of past wars.[68] Out of this awareness new statements have been issued.[69] From the wealth of material available we quote only one sampling:

> The levying of war taxes is another form of conscription which, along with the conscription of manpower, makes war possible. We are accountable to God for the use of our financial resources and should protest the use of our taxes in the promotion and waging of war. We stand by those who feel called to resist the payment of that portion of taxes being used for military purposes.[70]

In response to the growing war tax concern, the Commission on Home Ministries of the General Conference Mennonite Church began publishing the *God and Caesar* newsletter in January of 1975. The mailing list has grown dramatically.[71] Peaceful tax paying is already a worldwide movement. Japanese leaders have experienced considerable support for a better way.[72] Thousands in the United States have declined to pay the federal telephone excise tax since 1966, including a few Mennonite and Church of the Brethren congregations. Most of these are seeking alternative uses for these funds. Legal research has been done by the Peacemaker Movement and the American Friends Service Committee.[73]

While there is this serious reexamination of the war tax issue, it must be remembered that many see no inconsistency between a commitment to Christian love and the payment of war taxes. Because of this diversity there is a need to cultivate a spirit of discernment where people are loved whether or not they agree with one another's approach to this ethical dilemma.

Too Much to Caesar, Too Little to God?

The annual United States budget is dominated by a hydra-headed military appropriation. The costs of technological weaponry are astronomical. And the amount Christians pay for things they know are absolutely evil is frightening. In 1959 it was estimated that the average American family paid $850 per year for military defense through taxes.[74] For fiscal 1977 it was estimated that "the average American family is taxed $1,600 annually to support the military program of a government that gave us Watergate, Vietnam, the CIA, and the largest nuclear stockpile in the world."[75] It should be no secret to anyone that Christians today pay more in taxes for the support of the military than they give voluntarily for the support of the church and other benevolent causes. Does this constitute defensible stewardship? Not if money represents something of our life energy. Can people really believe that they are advancing the cause of Christ when they hand over more money to pay for war than they give to heal the wounds of the world? Schizophrenic giving describes it best. War taxes are a tremendous waste of resources. They are in fact a theft from those who hunger and are not fed, those who are cold and not clothed. The militaristic budget of death reveals that stewardship is a fearfully neglected aspect of the gospel in our time.[76]

Killing Via the Tax Method

In view of the increased sensitivity about the business of paying for war let us identify two of the ways in which citizens are implicated in war taxes.

1. The excise tax on telephone service is the most explicit tax for war in the United States. It has been associated with war spending since 1914. It was reinstated in 1966 to help pay for the Vietnam war. Congressman Wilbur Mills said, "It is clear that the Vietnam operation and only the Vietnam operation makes this bill necessary."[77] And Senator Frank Church confirmed that "when all the rhetoric is stripped away (this added tax) is simply a war tax."[78] "That last phone bill was a real killer!" the posters stated. No fooling. The Federal excise tax has helped to make certain that thousands of people will never use the telephone.

2. The Federal income tax and particularly the system of withholding income at the source provide funds for war. Defense spending in the United States has escalated to 40 and 70 percent of the national budget. The money for this budget of death is conscripted through the federal income tax—the chief link connecting each indi-

vidual's daily labor with the continuing buildup for war. It is absolutely frightening to contemplate the enormous sums of money which Christians have been paying for war. With one hand we give generously for life-building purposes, and with the other we cancel out the good that we have done by allowing the secular power to conscript an even larger amount of money for the destruction of human life. Who will deliver us from this death—from rendering unto Caesar that which is not his?

The federal income tax became possible in 1913 when the sixteenth amendment to the Constitution was adopted. Prior to that time the Supreme Court frequently challenged the constitutionality of revenue acts. It is believed that the Civil War (1861-65) accelerated the development of income taxation. The first income tax in the United States was imposed under Lincoln in 1862 when the costs of the Civil War were resulting in an increase of the public debt by as much as two million dollars per day. The tax was abolished ten years later.

The withholding system of tax collection in the United States first became law in June 1943. At that time only 10 percent of the population paid income taxes. The shift from a "class tax" to a "pay-as-you-earn mass tax" was necessitated by the tremendous cost of weapons during World War II. Two fifths of the total cost of the war was paid for out of these taxes, and the number of persons liable was raised between 1939 and 1943 from four to thirty million. Through this indirect method of withholding the government enforces collection through employers who are the unsalaried agents of the Internal Revenue Service. In reality the withholding tax is legal confiscation at the source of income for every employed citizen (with few exceptions). This arrangement undermines responsibility and makes it very difficult for the average citizen to exercise control over a portion of his own salary. In our time it seems almost natural for us to open our pocketbooks and checkbooks to every official demand of the State. Yet this was not true in the United States prior to 1913.

Signs of Hope in a Warring World

The Society of Friends, the Church of the Brethren, and more recently the Mennonites have invested time and energy urging the United States government to provide a nonmilitary arrangement for meeting tax obligations. For centuries peace church members have paid military taxes even though they refused to bear arms themselves.

> Now, as the artificiality of the distinction between arms and paying for others to bear them has become so shockingly clear, more and more of our members are refusing to pay some or all of the taxes that support the military budget.
> ... Many are now finding this choice so intolerable that they, as well as many tax resisters, are working for legislation which would give taxpayers who are conscientious objectors the same kind of consideration that has traditionally been given to draftees who are conscientious objectors.[79]

Two plans deserve special mention:

(1) *The Civilian Income Tax Fund.* During the early 1960s the Pacific Yearly Meeting of Friends circulated a proposed bill offering a tax alternative. Conscientious objectors would have designated their tax money for the support of the United Nations International Children's Emergency Fund (UNICEF). Some were offering to pay an additional 5 percent above their normally computed

51

tax as a proof of their sincerity. The Church of the Brethren was urging the formation of specific non-military accounts to overcome the problem of a common treasury. It was assumed that unless citizens can vote for peace as well as war with their money we still have "taxation without representation" 200 years after Independence.

(2) *The World Peace Tax Fund Act.* In a further effort to channel tax money into life-sustaining programs rather than into weapons of death, the World Peace Tax Fund Act was introduced in the House of Representatives in April 1972. It has been reintroduced annually since then as well as introduced in the Senate in 1977. If enacted the bill would establish a special trust fund and thus allow the military portion of federal taxes to be used for peaceful purposes.

The WPTF effort to obtain a legal alternative began in 1971 with a group of concerned citizens in Ann Arbor, Michigan, including some from the University of Michigan law school. For the sake of their own integrity they wanted to be freed from the requirement to kill anyone through any means, including taxation. Their purpose was to allow the citizen to redirect his taxes, not avoid them.

A National Council for a World Peace Tax Fund was organized in 1975 to promote the enactment of legislation which would grant people a legal alternative to the payment of war taxes. "Taxes for Peace Not War" is their slogan. It is doubtful that this goal will be achieved easily but there are indicators that it is a realistic one. If sufficient support develops in each state and people take the initiative to inform their congresspersons of the need for this act, the desired legislation could become law. The

Act would have great appeal to all those who feel that they are being penalized when they follow their own consciences because they are forced by law to finance multibillion dollar weapons programs. Not only would this Act give citizens the choice of voting for peace or for war, it would also help us to preserve the freedoms which the Constitution and the Bill of Rights attempt to guarantee. The idea of giving citizens tax relief for their conscientious objections to war is likely to be around for a long time.

A Peace Tax Has Its Limits

The World Peace Tax Fund Act is not an unmixed blessing. Phil M. Shenk has done a remarkable service in warning that the WPTF may not be the most faithful response to a warmongering world. He asks whether the legitimization of objection to war would strengthen the protest or whether it would mortally wound personal conviction and severely weaken social impact. Whenever the state claims to respect the consciences of those persons opposing war, Shenk feels it tends to dilute the church's prophetic voice against the world's ungodly love for war. The early church was seduced in this way by the Roman emperor Constantine's legalization of the church. Its strength was sapped, its faith made tolerant by tolerance. Special niches and legal exemptions tended to foster reclusive passivity.

Would the legal alternative in the WPTF be more responsible than tax resistance? Shenk is doubtful. He believes the church's faithful response should include both positive action and negative protest. In other words, church members can protest by refusing to pay war taxes and at the same time promote peace positively by giving time and money to peace projects. Both dimensions are necessary for a balanced peace agenda. Phil Shenk contends that the church necessarily confronts a world at odds with its values. In contrast to military budgets the church upholds a value system founded on the love of Christ. Consequently,

> . . . worldly priorities must be objected to in word and deed. If the objecting deeds are performed legally, they register little if any protest. If consciously illegal, they register an unequivocal refusal to agree with world's values. The latter gets the attention of the state, the former does not.
>
> Simple tax resistance would free the church to spend its energies calling the whole world to salvation rather than saving just itself.
>
> The church's "in-ness" but "not-of-ness" demands that it be actively concerned about the nonchurched world. Christ as Lord is subject to no other authority. Because of this, the church's most crucial task is to prophetically and faithfully enact and promote Christ's values in life without regard for political limitations or definitions. The politics of Jesus are not those of compromise, but those of dogged, active, and consistent faithfulness.[80]

For this reason MCC Peace Section recommends that people continue to work toward reduction of military spending, not resting content with special war tax exemption privileges. Any resistance to war and to those authorities which bring about war is not a negative presence. The fact is that every no implies a yes, and this *no* to killing and death can be a *yes* to healing and life. War tax resistance is a process filled with hope. It can curb the expansion of the military. While radical tax resistance may be a more courageous response than working for a special fund devoted to nonmilitary purposes, should we not welcome every effort which seeks to be faithful to the self-giving love of God revealed in Christ?

For Those Who Like a Challenge

Paying taxes is a deeply ingrained habit in the lives of most American citizens. In spite of our inclination to be tax-paying, law-abiding citizens, and despite the complexity of the war tax issue we do not need to be helpless in the face of this evil. Each of us has viable options which we can use to register our faithfulness to Jesus Christ as Lord and our opposition to corporate war making by the state within which we live. Following are methods which persons are using to say "no" to war taxes, and "yes" to taxes for peace:

(1) Engage people in conversation on this issue wherever you go and employ all legal means available to correct the injustice of war tax demands.

Paul Leatherman of Pennsylvania is a prime example of a Christian who energetically and cheerfully reaches out to persons to explore war tax options. God has given him a love for people and he welcomes every opportunity to build support for his deep ethical concern about human life. To achieve this objective he engages IRS representatives in conversation and invites them to eat meals with his family.

Are we inclined to overlook the power of persuasion which God has given to each of us? Yet every significant idea or conviction which people hold had a small beginning. The same is true for the war tax issue. Seeds of concern or awareness planted three or four decades ago have taken root and resulted in alternative movements. With imagination and persistence it might well be that a

Tax Fund for Peace could be developed. If citizens distribute leaflets, write letters to newspapers, and speak forth for new possibilities, our goal could become a reality. The separation of church and state does not mean that Christians have nothing to say to, or ask of, the state, but rather that the state cannot ask everything of them. We need not be afraid to ask for religious liberty even when we think that the powers that be are disinclined to grant it. Let us use the power of the written and spoken word. (See Appendix D).

(2) *Discontinue the voluntary payment of the federal excise tax on telephone service.* In 1966 this tax, as explicitly a war tax as any that United States citizens are asked to pay, was raised to 10 percent primarily to help pay for the war costs in Vietnam. Those who have chosen to resist the payment of war taxes have found the withholding of funds to be a simple, direct, and an effective way of letting government leaders know how they feel. At the height of resistance to the Indochina War, it was estimated there were 200,000 telephone tax resisters. Because telephone companies are not happy serving as tax collecting agents for the government they frequently give citizens support in their opposition to the tax. The tax, although small in comparison to the federal income tax, does give people a handle whereby they can be heard within a democratic structure.

At the present time it is easy to determine the amount of money which goes for the tax on the monthly telephone bill. It is designated as "U.S. Tax." People who deduct the amount from their payment generally include a postcard or letter to the telephone company along with their check or money order. Periodically, they also inform the Internal Revenue Service of the reasons behind their action. One note reads as follows:

> I do not support the priorities of our government which emphasize arms buildup at the expense of human needs. Therefore, I have deducted from my telephone bill the $_____ federal tax.
>
> The federal excise tax on phone service has been raised and lowered periodically since World War II depending on our country's military involvement. This war tax represents a continuing reliance on military force to protect American corporate interests abroad and therefore I can not in good conscience pay for it.[81]

Generally the risk of refusing is small even though the IRS does speak about substantial fine and prison penalties. It seems that the IRS does not want the publicity which develops when people are arrested for refusing to pay this war tax. David H. Janzen of Newton, Kansas, discovered the witness potential of this appraoch in 1972 when friends rallied to his support at the IRS's public auction of his automobile.[82] Telephone tax refusal is a small act in which money talks. It can provide a clear demonstration to people and to governments that Christians are indeed serious about following Jesus.

(3) Increase your contributions for missions and service (tax deductible causes). The IRS code of the United States government does permit citizens the option of giving up to 30 percent and sometimes even 50 percent of their income to charitable purposes. This means in effect that people can reduce their taxable income by increasing their giving.

Levi Keidel is convinced, however, that Mennonites today build their lifestyles around selected parts of their heritage (i.e., holy living, evangelism, voluntary poverty, or nonviolence) and thereby seriously erode the credibility of their Christian witness to people. To illustrate, Keidel writes:

> ... We Mennonites who have set our affection upon things of earth, relished the pleasures and the conveniences of affluence, amassed material wealth like everyone else, now say that we will refuse to pay income tax as our peace witness to government. We are selecting to apply the principle of nonparticipation in violence, but not of self-imposed poverty for the sake of the kingdom of heaven.[83]

Most Christians fail to reach the standard of a tithe in their giving. In this respect refusing to pay war taxes has proven to be a blessing for many people and for many church-related causes. Attempts to make a living without being subject to war taxes have resulted in some people finding or backing into a simple lifestyle.[84] It has helped them to reorder their priorities. Those with large incomes have discovered that they could give more and live on less. For them the simple life is more healthful, more joyful, and more blessed in every way. By responding more generously to the needs of the poor they have experienced the joy of contributing to life, not death. If their monetary resources are not used for killing perhaps then decision-makers will take more seriously their concern to have their tax money channeled into life-sustaining programs rather than into weapons of death. As a single person, Cornelia Lehn of Newton, Kansas, is among those who has selected this option of giving more in order to reduce her complicity in war.[85]

(4) Limit your income to a nontaxable level. Most people choose not to live below the taxable line as this would be taking on a standard of living dictated by

government. Others, again, would rather live in "poverty" than break tax laws. For them it is an opportunity to begin living more simply, withdrawing further from consumerism and the war economy. (As one person observed, "Being a tax resister is like being poor—it's a good thing but so inconvenient!") Those who adopt this low-income style of life to avoid tax liability usually seek part-time work, short-term jobs, or limited self-employment. Such a lifestyle represents a sacrificial position financially. However, it is a significant form of witness and is "safe" within the limits of law (not civil disobedience, but accommodation to the law). Eldon and Helen Bargen of Elkhart, Indiana, have been practicing this strategy of war tax protest.

One of the attractive aspects of this strategy is that it permits one to work for an organization or employer who ordinarily cooperates with the IRS by withholding the tax supposedly due from the employee. The form may be signed by any employee who did not have tax liability for the previous year and expects to incur none in the current year. Although it must be signed anew in each calendar year, the form permits the employer to pay the full salary or wage without withholding taxes. Whether this method of tax resistance is for you or not, it certainly keeps money out of military hands!

The W-4E option, while no longer in general use, enables individuals to challenge effectively the vast power being brought to bear by governments on the lives of human beings. As *The Peacemaker* put it:

> One person, by changing himself in accordance with what he deeply believes, begins, at least in a small way, to change the world. Although great social changes are not

likely to come about from the effort of a single individual, no significant change can be made without the effort of each of us.[86]

Persons involved in intentional communities are discovering this to be a very satisfying, corporate way of challenging private ownership and accumulated wealth while maintaining a spirit of togetherness and community solidarity. Reba Place Fellowship in Evanston, Illinois, and the Fairview House in Wichita, Kansas, operate as "religious associations" under IRS Code Number 501-D.

(5) *Claim additional dependents to eliminate withholding.* This is achieved by refiling the W-4 form so that less or no tax is withheld by the employer. (Note: If one claims no tax liability for the previous year, one can also file a W-4 form to eliminate all withholding. Simply enter the word "Exempt" on Line 3.)

Because of the need to be known as persons of integrity the "W-4 resistance" strategy is not always acceptable to Christians. Also persons using this method are more vulnerable for prosecution than with most other methods. However, a change in the law in 1972 now permits people to claim extra exemptions without claiming false numbers of dependents. It is also possible to claim allowances by estimating itemized deductions in advance. Ivan and Rachel Friesen of Swift Current, Saskatchewan, engaged in W-4 refusal during 1972-1973. Finally the taxes which they had consistently refused to pay were confiscated from Rachel's paycheck by the IRS in 1976.[87]

If the tax system of the United States Government is truly based on voluntary compliance, it would be helpful if the Government would be more responsive to how peacemakers feel about the confiscation of citizens' earnings against their moral convictions.

(6) Claim a war tax credit (deduction) or a "refund of taxes illegally, erroneously, or excessively collected."

It may be a surprise to some that there is such a legal channel for recovering money which is intended for the Pentagon. There are two methods and both are very useful to those who are caught in the tax withholding system by virtue of their employment.

(a) One approach is to claim a "war crimes deduction" on "Schedule A—Itemized Deductions" of Form 1040 to bring the taxable income to a desired level. This method has been used successfully by Dr. and Mrs. Joseph Eigner of St. Louis, Missouri,[88] and James R. Klassen of Goessel, Kansas. It relies on a claim that one is not obligated to pay for war or for war crimes which may be based upon the First Amendment right to refuse dollar-participation in war for conscience' sake and/or the Nuremburg Principles which assert that "individual human beings are responsible for their acts." This method makes the allowances of the W-4 claim consistent and shows that the W-4 form is not fradulent.

(b) Another approach is to file for a refund using IRS Form 843. This claim form entitles citizens to call for a "refund of taxes illegally, erroneously, or excessively collected." It is available to any citizen who wishes to recover paid taxes. Claims may be filed within three years from the date of payment. In the 1960s noted folk singer-pacifist Joan Baez made this claim with the IRS, requesting that 60 percent of her withheld tax be returned.[89] Taxpayers Against War feel this strategy has several advantages: it is within the law, the government does not get additional money in penalties to purchase more weapons, and it allows the person who has taxes withheld (and therefore can't refuse payment) to protest in a significant way without experiencing a sort of constant niggling harassment that is dehumanizing and which finally is in direct opposition to the spirit of the witness.

Whether or not these two closely related methods achieve the goal of diverting money from the military they do provide us with another means of making a Christian witness to our society about the proper use of tax monies. We believe the effort is not wasted.

(7) Pay taxes under protest. Persons who are not prepared to refuse payment on a portion or all of their income taxes can certainly exercise the freedom to include a letter along with their payment. These cards and letters should be directed to the Internal Revenue Service with copies also going to congresspersons, the secretary of Tax Legislation, and the president. By paying under protest one is able to represent his views to the state without incurring the penalties that accompany the nonpayment of taxes. During the 1960s the Women's International League for Peace and Freedom made available a blue sticker which read: "That part of this income tax which is levied for preparation for war is paid only under protest." Since 1977 the National Council of the World Peace Tax Fund Act has circulated cards and encouraged citizens to engage in a write-in campaign to their representatives. Through this effort they expect to facilitate a growing Christian witness to government on the stewardship of money—to promote better ways of living instead of better ways of killing.

(8) Decline to pay or to cooperate with IRS attempts to collect taxes. This strategy necessitates earning a tax-

able income outside of the withholding system. There are types of work which do not come under the withholding rule of the IRS. Although exempt from withholding, such jobs are not exempt from tax, so people in these jobs have prime opportunity to refuse to pay. Ammon Hennacy of Utah is an example of a person who felt himself to be violated by the introduction of the withholding system. To preserve a small part of his morality, he quit his job and worked as a transient for eleven years, rather than pay taxes for war.[90] John Howard Yoder believes that at times,

> ... the most effective way to take responsibility is to refuse to collaborate. ... This refusal is not a withdrawal from society. It is rather a negative intervention within the process of social change, a refusal to use unworthy means even for what seems to be a worthy end.[91]

Nonpayment involves civil disobedience—refusing to obey a government order. This is an area of some controversy and involves risks. The refusal of conscientious objectors to become a part of the military during World War I was a significant factor in the ultimate development of the alternative service programs of World War II. It is this historical precedent which gives credence to these present-day alternatives to war taxes. Some tax refusers are convinced that nothing short of the most intense pressure will ever bring about change in anything as unyielding as the military establishment.

(9) File a 1040 Form but pay taxes selectively. Some persons calculate the percentage of the federal budget which is used for military purposes (i.e., 40 to 70 percent or a more precise figure) and then deduct that amount from their payment. Many persons choose voluntarily to

contribute the withheld portion to charities, peace organizations or UNICEF as a positive expression of their convictions. This method is useful when part of one's tax has been withheld from one's salary, and the IRS is claiming more, or if one is self-employed and owes IRS money. Obviously, self-employed persons not subject to withholding may do this more readily than those employed by a firm. The objection to this strategy is that the same proportion of what one does pay will still go for war preparations. Still, there is a world of difference between handing money over to the IRS without question and making them come seize it.

Refusal to pay these taxes subjects one to possible criminal prosecution by the government. Experiences vary but generally it can be stated that the government is more interested in collecting taxes than pressing criminal charges.[92] True, those who actively resist war taxes will discover that eventually the money can be taken by the IRS and the military, yet not without sparking some public interest and provoking numerous forums in which to voice one's concern. This has been the experience of Stan and Janet Reedy of Elkhart, Indiana, after deciding not to pay voluntarily 60 percent of their income tax. They are prepared to stop redirecting their tax money when the government reorders its priorities in favor of life over death. Jack Cady of Port Townsend, Washington, has also made his witness in a similar manner.[93]

(10) *Notify your employer of your conscientious objector stance on war taxes and request that such taxes not be withheld.* The employer will usually claim there is nothing he can do. (This was true for Cornelia Lehn, cited earlier.) However, there is always some value in having raised the issue. In an effort to challenge "the

64

threshold of legality" the American Friends Service Committee has worked energetically to protect and to promote the religious freedom of its employees. Louis W. Schneider stated:

> . . . As an organization we have always paid our taxes, but we are vehemently opposed to being compelled to act as tax collector against the conscience of employees. We believe that the employee has the right to confront the government directly on this issue and we should not be made to play the role of middleman.[94]

A. J. Muste (1885-1967) observed that if a tax refuser

> has a bank account or is earning wages or salary, the government can quite readily collect the money. At that point, the question arises whether temporary refusal to pay is more than a gesture, which gives one some inner satisfaction but achieves no social purpose, especially since "tax refusal" on this level—or perhaps on any—may have little or no actual economic effect. To this question one may answer that it is still much better *especially in a society which is geared to inducing conformity and making protest difficult,* to register some protest which makes one's neighbors, and also the public . . . pause and think, than it is to let the hideous business of collecting billions for nuclear war purposes go on smoothly without a voice being raised against it at the crucial moment when payment is demanded.[95]

(11) File a blank return. Using this strategy, people submit either a 1040 or 1040A form with their name and address at the top and their signature at the bottom, but nothing more. An attached letter explains that they consider themselves protected by the Fifth Amendment, as providing financial information could be evidence of

complicity in war crimes. The IRS may try to set a figure on the tax owed and then attempt to collect it.

(12) Refuse to file. There are those, like A. J. Muste of New York, who choose not to file a report at all. However uncompromising his stand appeared to be, it was observed that "when a man as respected as A. J. refuses to pay taxes, it's like Jeremiah walking down the street naked. People stop, look, and listen."[96] Muste's decision to pay *no* income tax was based on the fact that a huge percentage of whatever one pays must be thought of as going for war purposes. Willful failure to file a return is punishable by up to a year in prison and a $10,000 fine, plus costs of prosecution. For eleven years beginning in 1944, Walter Gormly of Mount Vernon, Iowa, reported his income but did not pay. He also then refused to file, because the IRS assessed penalties for not filing as a result of his refusal to sign the statement swearing to the return's accuracy.[97]

There are other options in addition to the twelve outlined above. Consult the handbooks for more information. To build a sense of community on the war tax issue it has been proposed that as many persons as possible withhold ten to twenty dollars of the federal income tax. An accompanying note would explain that this small token is a natural consequence the military must suffer for having such an oversized budget. It would also explain how this money would be used to meet human needs. Based on people's experience with the phone tax this approach would be unlikely to result in any legal proceedings. However, this shared experience would communicate a valid concern which could have empowering effects for the participants. This action would be symbolic, of course. Estimates of *real* dollars going to war purposes vary between 40 and 55 percent of the Congressionally controllable federal budget.[98]

In Solitary Witness

As we noted in the life of Henry David Thoreau, the individual's witness is not to be disparaged. Franz Jägerstätter, a relatively untutored farmer living in a remote village of Austria during Adolf Hitler's time of political power, wrestled with basic vocational questions. On the basis of his New Testament readings he experienced conflict in trying to satisfy simultaneously the demands of the community of God and the Nazi folk community. Definitely preferring to preserve his rights granted under the kingdom of God, Jägerstätter deliberately refused military service in Hitler's army. For this act of dissent he was imprisoned and finally beheaded on August 9, 1943.

The account of this modern saint is the more remarkable because he was able to reach this decision without the support of family, friends, or his own religious community. He rejected the plea from each of them to bend and therefore survive. Inspired by the Scriptures and the Holy Spirit this heroic peasant went knowingly to his death. Determined to be loyal to God he confronted his Caesar with a good conscience. By meditation and prayer God led this man, who tested in life what he heard in his conscience, along a difficult but good path.

In retrospect we see this costly discipleship of Jesus as being good for others as well as for Jägerstätter himself. Faint-hearted obedience to Hitler could never have compensated him for the satisfaction of doing the will of the Almighty.[99] Jägerstätter's experience underscores the fact that "we must learn to live with social alienation since it is part of the price for recalling one another to the demands of the (Christian) covenant."[100] The individual conscience against the demonic powers. There is no other way.

Refusing the Old Powers

Not all of us are able to make our Christian witness alone as Franz Jägerstätter did. Although it is often said that "God and I are a majority" most of us need the support of persons who care. A prophet needs a fellowship base; a dissenter needs a caring community. Most of us need to band together for courage and action. Perhaps Christopher Fry caught the feeling in the character Tim Meadows:

> Dark and cold we may be, but this
> Is no winter now. The frozen misery
> Of centuries breaks, cracks, begins to move,
> The thunder is the thunder of the foes,
> The thaw, the flood, the upstart Spring.
> Thank God our time is now when wrong
> Comes up to face us everywhere,
> Never to leave us till we take
> The longest stride of soul men ever took.
> Affairs are now soul size.
> The enterprise
> Is exploration into God.
> Where are you going? It takes
> So many thousand years to wake,
> But will you wake for pity's sake,
> Pete's sake, Dave or one of you,
> Wake up, will you? . . .[101]

The need to get our Christian faith off the level of talk and writing and onto the level of action is imperative.

But the difficulty of achieving this objective is clarified for us by Doug Hostetter:

> For 400 years we Mennonites have had a theology of complete peace and noncooperation in war. But the fact is we have been at war with the Vietnamese. We have paid our taxes which have bought the bombs that have killed the people. We have cooperated with Selective Service even when we have not gone into the military. We have said if there is conflict between Christ and the government, we choose Christ. But in the last fifty years we have never felt we had to make a decision against the government. [102]

That is a serious indictment of our failure to practice the gospel we hear and preach. Unless Christians recognize the interrelatedness of money and the military we will discover to our dismay that the graves of our dead enemies will have been dug with the coins engraved, "In God We Trust." What blasphemy! Will we continue indefinitely to sin against God with "our" property? Will the "authorities" forever intimidate us in our witness for Christ? Will there always be a contradiction in our lives—a profession of allegiance to the Prince of Peace and a denial of it in our tax payments for war?

Let us hope that the values on which we base our lives will make the paying of war taxes an obvious impossibility. Could the Holy Spirit prevent our hands from writing checks that go for war and motivate us to write more checks for peace and justice? Could we tell the tax collector in action clear enough for all the world to see that we have committed ourselves to LIFE? The sixteenth-century Anabaptists have given us a model to emulate.

They simply refused the old powers and institutions the authority which they were claiming over people. They began to live as though the kingdom of God, whose final arrival they anticipated, had already fully come. They said in their day "the war is over," and commenced to live in peace.[103]

There is further precedent for this model in the testimony and ethical worship of the first-century church. With the fear of the Lord before their eyes they asserted their deep commitment to love: "When anyone is united to Christ, there is a new world; the old order has gone, and a new order has already begun" (2 Corinthians 5:17, NEB). Is it any wonder, then, that John Woolman recognized "the advantage of living in the real substance of religion, where practice doth harmonize with principle"?[104]

Will we who live in the twentieth century also issue the call to living and acting as though the old institutions no longer tyranize? Who will perform a death-defying act? The choice is up to us. Because her church believes in the way of peace, Cornelia Lehn wants all to stand up in horror and refuse to help the government to make war, declaring, "We will not give you our sons and daughters and we will not give you our money to kill others."[105] "Dealing with a problem of this proportion will be costly," John Drescher has warned.

It may demand a different lifestyle, the loss of property and institutions. We can be assured, however, that the way of obedience, even though it leads through the wilderness and death, is the way of Christ. Out of death we believe there is always a resurrection. And how our world needs resurrection life![106]

70

In the words of Melvin Schmidt, the prophetic tax refuser

> measures his action only in terms of God's ultimate purpose for the world and the radical demands of Christ. An analogous situation is the case of the pacifist who is charged by his compatriots with not being a "good patriot" because of his refusal to bear arms. The pacifist rejects the criterion of the other citizens and sees himself as being a "good patriot" for entirely different, and higher, reasons. Likewise, prophetic tax refusal is not a denial of responsibility for the social situation, but acceptance of it in a personal encounter with evil.[107]

One Act of Dedication

The struggles of Jesus are ours too. Like Him, it is our task to unmask the subtle idolatries. Like Him too, we take our cues from history, but our call from beyond history. Interestingly enough, Jesus found a way of meeting at once the claims of Caesar and those of God. He was not torn between the two. The way He put it together, there is only one act of dedication which fulfills the demand of Caesar and the demand of God. That act is obedience to God even to the point of death. (See Philippians 2:8).

Anyone who embarks on such a course must be prepared for the fiery furnace—or the cross. Actually, Jesus' death on the cross is the model of what it means to render to Caesar what is Caesar's and to God what is God's. Apparently, Jesus did not think that His aggressive confrontation with the Jewish authorities violated the law of love. Instead it suggested that love can and should take certain forms of resistance. Because of conflicting values, Caesar eventually demanded of Jesus His life, and Jesus paid it. In doing this His life was simultaneously in a much profounder sense given to God. As Marlin Jeschke points out, Jesus' life and death is finally the best interpretation and answer to the question about paying taxes.

> . . . Caesar may rob us of our money as he may rob us of our life. But these, both money and life, are really God's. With Jesus we must start with the act of devoting them to the kingdom. This then exposes Caesar as the invader that he is, whose taxation of people may actually be an act of plunder.
>
> The problem for many people whose conscience bothers them about paying taxes is that they have somehow accepted the state system too positively. They have forgotten the fallenness and rapaciousness of Caesar. And they have perhaps also forgotten that the discipled community is a radical alternative.[108]

Strange as it seems, good news is seldom perceived as such. Therefore, Jesus' disciples must be prepared for rejection and persecution.

Although Jesus never became a Zealot (a militant revolutionary) he was condemned to death as a Zealot by the Romans. This insight tells us that we must be willing to be understood by others in a less favorable, more revolutionary way than we understand ourselves. In our opposition to war taxes, Willard Swartley believes that

> we must accept the liability that political forces will brand both our resistance and nonresistance as revolutionary. But it might just well be that this discrepancy between their perception and our self-understanding is the critical test of our faithfulness to the ethic of Jesus.[109]

In the Nuclear Age the institutions of war are not only

murderous of persons but of human existence itself. To help them thrive by means of one's life, whether that life be spent in military service or in the payment of heavy war taxes, is to sow death across mankind's future. Therefore, to be freed from the clutches of a war economy might be the most appropriate act of repentance for us to do. But it could be a costly discipleship. It will happen only when we join the Lamb's War—when we commit ourselves to the task of incarnating the Jesus lifestyle of servanthood. To render to Caesar the things that are Caesar's is to bear in mind always that it was Caesar's cross on which Jesus died so that "the Christian, too, may finally have to render to Caesar a cross rather than a denarius."[110]

> . . . We could succeed in not paying taxes and still miss the kingdom. We could also fail in resisting tax payment and *also* fail to have taken up the life of the kingdom. . . .[111]

Our task then, individually and corporately, is to "render to Caesar the things that are Caesar's," but above all to "give to God what is His, perhaps in conflict with everything else."[112] Martin Buber has assured us that "those who know God dare dread no earthly power."[113]

Claiming God's Ability to Do the Impossible

Not everything that needs to be done on the war tax problem is illegal. But if it is illegal it certainly "is a high crime to break the laws of Jesus Christ in order to yield obedience to earthly rulers."[114] God help us to throw off our timidity, and with courage, joy, and boldness to act more meaningfully. Recognizing the principalities and powers at work in our world, let us, like discriminating disciples of the past, be selective in the taxes we agree to pay.[115] May God arm our respective communities with such inner strength that we will need no military weapons for defense or for expansion. Fortunately,

> God never fails to offer the strength to deal with the consequences of following His will. This is a fundamental part of His covenant with persons. With God's love, we are truly liberated from the limitations of this world.[116]

> Having no gift of strategy, no arms,
>   No secret weapon and no walled defense,
>   I shall become a citizen of love,
> That little nation with the blood-stained sod
> Where even the slain have power, the only country
>   That sends forth an ambassador to God.
> Renouncing self and crying out to evil
>   To end its wars, I seek a land that lies
>   All unprotected like a sleeping child.
>   Nor is my journey reckless and unwise.
> Who doubts that love has an effective weapon
>   May meet with a surprise.[117]

God's amazing love can make possible creative responses to seemingly impossible situations—even the impossible task of resolving the war tax problem. As we trust the Holy Spirit we too will find solutions, some conventional and some unconventional. Seeking first His kingdom, and accepting this problem as a gift of God, we are therefore able to live. Jesus said:

> Happy are those who work for peace;
>   God will call them his children!
> Happy are those who are persecuted because they do what
>   God requires; the Kingdom of heaven belongs to them!
> —Matthew 5:9, 10, TEV.

NOTES AND REFERENCES

1. Jeanette Rankin, first woman in Congress and the only member of Congress to vote against both World Wars. Quoted by David Wood in "Militarism: A $10-A-Week Habit" (122 W. Franklin Ave., Minneapolis, Minn.: Minnesota Clergy & Laity Concerned), p. 1.

2. Staughton Lynd (editor), *Nonviolence in America: A Documentary History* (New York: Bobbs-Merrill, 1966), p. xxxiii.

3. Nat Hentoff (editor), *The Essays of A. J. Muste* (Indianapolis, New York, and Kansas City: The Bobbs-Merrill, 1967), p. 371.

4. Will Durant and Ariel Durant, *The Lessons of History* (3533 W. Pico Blvd., Los Angeles, Calif., 90019: S & S Enterprises, 1968).

5. Donald D. Kaufman, *What Belongs to Caesar?* (Scottdale, Pa.: Herald Press, 1969; 1973 Revised Bibliography), p. 31.

6. Frank H. Epp, "On the topic of the tax," *The Mennonite* (March 7, 1961), p. 151.

7. Donald F. Durnbaugh (editor), *The Brethren in Colonial America* (Elgin, Ill.: The Brethren Press, 1967), pp. 364-5; John C. Wenger, *History of the Mennonites of the Franconia Conference* (Telford, Pa.: Franconia Mennonite Historical Society, 1937), p. 410; and John C. Wenger, *Pacifism and Biblical Nonresistance* (Scottdale, Pa.: Herald Press, 1968), p. 26.

8. Dale W. Brown, "The Bible on Tax Resistance," *Sojourners* (March, 1977), pp. 13-14.

9. John Howard Yoder, "The Things That Are Caesar's" (Part I), *Christian Living* (July, 1960), p. 5; *The Christian Witness to the State* (Newton, Kan.: Faith and Life Press, 1964), p. 75; and *The Politics of Jesus* (Grand Rapids, Mich.: Eerdmans, 1972), pp. 163-214.

10. Robert Friedmann, "Claus Felbinger's Confession of 1560," *Mennonite Quarterly Review*, XXIX (April, 1955), p. 145, and Walter Klaassen, "Mennonites and War Taxes," p. 3 (mimeographed) p. 5 (printed edition, Newton, Kans.: Faith and Life Press, 1978) portions were first presented to the Mennonite War Tax Conference held at Kitchener, Ontario, on November 1, 1975.

11. The quotation is by an unnamed participant in a 1977 consultation on the draft and national service held in Kansas City, Mo. (Bulletin # 4782, Faith and Life Press, North Newton, Kans.: 67117).

12. *The Interpreter's Bible* and numerous other commentaries: Commission on Home Ministries (GCMC) "Resource Packet on Civil Reponsibility," Elkhart, Indiana, Consultation, June 1-4, 1978 (Box 347, Newton, Kans.: 67114, Cost: $1.50)

Brown, Dale W. "Some Possibilities for a Biblical Case for Tax Refusal," *Brethren Life and Thought*, Vol. XIX (Spring, 1974) pp. 101-112.

Cranfield, C. E. B., *A Commentary on Romans 12—13.*

Cullmann, Oscar, *The State in the New Testament.*

Durnbaugh, Donald F. (ed.) *On Earth Peace* (Discussions on War/Peace Issues Between Friends, Mennonites, Brethren, and European Churches, 1935-75).

Eller, Vernard, *King Jesus' Manual of Arms for the Armless* (War and Peace from Genesis to Revelation).

Fast, Henry A., *Jesus and Human Conflict.*

Kaufman, Donald D., *What Belongs to Caesar?* (esp. chapters II & III).

Keeney, William, "Fighting Like Heaven"

Kehler, Larry, *The Rule of the Lamb.*

Kennard, J. Spencer, Jr., *Render to God.*

Kraybill, Donald B., *Our Star-Spangled Faith* (esp. chapter 10) and *The Upside-Down Kingdom.*

Kuenning, Larry, *Exiles in Babylon.*

Lasserre, Jean, *War and the Gospel.*

Macgregor, G. H. C., *The New Testament Basis of Pacifism* (Revised Edition).

Rutenber, Culbert G., *The Dagger and the Cross.*

Swartley, Willard, "The Christian and Payment of War Taxes" (mimeographed study presented to the Mennonite War Tax Conference held at Kitchener, Ontario, on November 1, 1975).

Trocmé, André, *Jesus and the Nonviolent Revolution.*

Yoder, John Howard, *The Christian Witness to the State* and *The Politics of Jesus.*

For additional bibliography see *What Belongs to Caesar?*, pp. 104-122.

13. William Stringfellow, *An Ethic for Christians and Other Aliens in a Strange Land* (Waco, Texas: Word Books, 1973), pp. 72-73.

14. The writer of Psalm 51 prays: "O Lord God, my deliverer, save me from bloodshed [or blood guiltiness], and I will sing the praises of thy justice" (verse 14, NEB). Also Isaiah (1:15b) reflects on God's attitude toward bloodshed: "Even though you make many prayers, I will not listen: your hands are full of blood."

15. John E. Steen, "Death and Taxes" leaflet (204½ W. Third St., Santa Ana, Calif.: Orange Country Peace and Human Rights Center, 1969).

16. Richard K. MacMaster, *Christian Obedience in Revolutionary Times: The Peace Churches and the American Revolution* (Akron,

Pa.: Mennonite Central Committee, Peace Section, 1976), p. 16 and John L. Ruth,'*Twas Seeding Time: A Mennonite View of the American Revolution* (Scottdale, Pa.: Herald Press, 1976), pp. 58-59.

17. John L. Ruth, *Ibid.*, p. 71.

18. *Ibid.*, p. 163.

19. Wilhelm Mensching, *Conscience* (Wallingford, Pa.: Pendle Hill Pamphlets by Sowers Printing Company, Lebanon, Pa., August, 1961), p. 15.

20. John M. Drescher, "Taxes for War" (an editorial), *Gospel Herald* (June 27, 1972), p. 545.

21. Kenneth Cragg in the introduction to M. Kamel Hussein's *City of Wrong: A Friday in Jerusalem* (Amsterdam, The Netherlands: N. V. Djambatan, 1959), p. xiv.

22. M. Kamel Hussein, *City of Wrong, op. cit.*, p. 68.

23. *Ibid.*, pp. 123-4.

24. Karl Menninger, *Whatever Became of Sin?* (New York: Hawthorne Books, Inc., 1973), p. 99.

25. For a more objective account covering a period of four centuries see the author's mimeographed article, "A Chronology of Wars Reflecting the 'Anabaptist' Response to War Taxes," first presented to the Mennonite War Tax Conference, Kitchener, Ontario, Canada, Oct. 30 to Nov. 1, 1975 (28 pages including footnotes).

26. Harold S. Bender, "Taxation," *Mennonite Encyclopedia*, Vol. IV (Scottdale, Pa.: Mennonite Publishing House, 1959), p. 688. See also Peter Brock, *Pacifism in Europe to 1914* (Princeton, N.J.: Princeton Unviersity Press), pp. 236-9, 243; Walter Klaassen, "Mennonites and War Taxes," *op. cit.*, pp. 10-11. (mimeographed), pp 12-13 (printed edition).

27. Robert Friedmann, "Claus Felbinger's Confession of 1560," *op. cit.*, p. 147, and Walter Klaassen, *Anabaptism: Neither Catholic nor Protestant* (Waterloo, Ont.: Conrad Press, 1973), p. 56.

28. Ernest R. Bomley, "The Case for Tax Refusal," *Fellowship* (November, 1974), p. 172.

29. Franklin Zahn (compiler), "Historical Notes on Conscience vs. War Taxes," p.1.

30. Guy F. Hershberger, *Nonresistance and the State* (Scottdale, Pa.: Mennonite Publishing House, 1937), p. 33. For a comprehensive account of the Quaker peace testimony see Peter Brock, *Pioneers of the Peaceable Kingdom* (Princeton, N.J.: Princeton University Press, 1968), 382 pages.

31. Isaac Sharpless, *A Quaker Experiment in Government* quoted in Melvin D. Schmidt, "Tax Refusal as Conscientious Objection to

War," *Mennonite Quarterly Review* Vol. XLIII (July, 1969), p. 234.

32. Janet Whitney (ed.), *The Journal of John Woolman* (Chicago, Ill.: Henry Regnery Company, 1950), pp. 66, 68.

33. Margaret E. Hirst, *The Quakers in Peace and War* (New York: George H. Doran Company, 1923), pp. 344-349, 367-382; and Donald F. Durnbaugh (editor), *The Brethren in Colonial America, op. cit.*, pp. 145-6.

34. Robert Calvert (compiler and editor), *Ain't Gonna Pay for War No More*, 2nd Edition (New York: War Tax Resistance, 1972), p. 37. And Peter Brock, *Pacifism in the United States: From the Colonial Era to First World War* (Princeton, N.J.: Princeton University Press, 1968), pp. 150-2. The official query of the Society of Friends periodically read in its Meetings was, "Are you faithful in maintaining our Christian testimony against all war as inconsistent with the precepts and spirit of the gospel?"

35. Donald F. Durnbaugh, *op. cit.*, p. 146.

36. John L. Ruth, *op. cit.*, pp. 64, 81-92; 162-195; and Richard K. MacMaster, *op. cit.*, p. 18. See also J. S. Hartzler and Daniel Kauffman, *Mennonite Church History* (Scottdale, Pa.: Mennonite Book and Tract Society, 1905), p. 165; "Christian Funk and the Schism Among the Mennonites. His Stand for Loyalty," *The Mennonite* (July 15, 1920), pp. 1-3; Guy F. Hershberger, *War, Peace, and Nonresistance* (Scottdale, Pa.: Herald Press, 1946), pp. 94-5; Millard Lind, *Answer to War* (Scottdale, Pa.: Herald Press, 1952), pp. 63-4; and William Warren Sweet, *The Story of Religion in America* (New York: Harper and Brothers, 1930, 1950), p. 187. Authors Ruth and Lind believe that Mennonites agonized over both the conflicting demands of two Caesars and the legitimacy of war tax payments.

37. Quoted by Donald F. Durnbaugh, *The Brethren in Colonial America, op. cit.*, pp. 364-5; and Wilbur Bender, *Nonresistance in Colonial Pennsylvania* (Scottdale, Pa.: Mennonite Publishing House, 1934), p. 18.

38. Peter M. Friesen, *The Mennonite Brotherhood in Russia* (1789-1910) Translated from the German. (Fresno, Calif.: Board of Christian Literature, G.C. of Mennonite Brethren Churches, 1978), pp 50, 87ff. Frank H. Epp, *Mennonites in Canada, 1786-1920; The History of a Separate People* (Toronto: Macmillan of Canada, 1974), p. 48; H. Penner, "West Prussian Mennonites Through Four Centuries," *Mennonite Quarterly Review*, XXIII (1949), pp. 242-3; John B. Toews, "The Origins and Activities of the Mennonite 'Selbstschutz' in the Ukraine" (1918-1919), *Mennonite Quarterly Review*, XLVI (January, 1972), p. 10; and Walter Klaassen, "Mennonites and War Taxes," *op. cit.*, p. 16. (mimeographed), p. 19 (printed edition).

39. Harold S. Bender, "Kleine Gemeinde," *Mennonite Encyclopedia*, Vol. III, p. 196; Paul Toews (editor), *Pilgrims and Strangers* (Essays in Mennonite Brethren History), (4824 E. Butler, Fresno, Calif. 93727: Center for Mennonite Brethren Studies, MBBS, 1977), pp. 58 and 62; John A. Toews, *A History of the Mennonite Brethren Church* (Fresno, Calif.: Board of Christian Literature, 1975), pp. 26-29; Mary Lou Cummings (editor), *Full Circle* (Newton, Kans.: Faith and Life Press, 1978), pp. 192 and 194.

40. Staughton Lynd (editor), *op. cit.*, pp. 41-2.

41. Lillian Schlissel (editor), *Conscience in America* (New York: E. P. Dutton & Co., Inc., 1968), p. 77.

42. Henry David Thoreau, *Walden* and *On the Duty of Civil Disobedience* (New York: Collier Books, 1962), esp. pp. 236-55; see also Ammon Hennacy, *The One-Man Revolution in America* (Salt Lake City, Utah: Ammon Hennacy Publications, 1970), pp. 68-88 and James Daugherty (editor), *Henry David Thoreau: A Man for Our Time* (New York: Viking Press, 1967).

43. Larry Gara, *War Resistance in Historical Perspective* (Wallingford, Pa.: Pendle Hill Pamphlets #171,1970), p.11; H.A. De Boer, *The Bridge Is Love* (London: Marshall, Morgan and Scott, 1957), p. 112.

44. Leo Tolstoy. *Writings on Civil Disobedience and Non-Violence* (New York: The New American Library, Inc., 1967), p. 23; Arthur and Lila Weinberg (ed.), *Instead of Violence* (Boston, Mass.: Beacon Press, 1963), p. 329.

45. Carl D. Soule, Review of *Conscientious Objection in the Civil War*, by Edward Needles Wright, *The Reporter for Conscience' Sake*, XIX (June, 1962), p. 2.

46. Guy F. Hershberger, *War, Peace, and Nonresistance, op. cit.*, p. 99; Peter Brock, *Pacifism in the United States, op. cit.*, p. 763.

47. *The Laws of the State of Kansas* passed at the Fourteenth Annual Session of the Legislature, commenced at the State Capital on Tuesday, Jan. 13, 1874 (Topeka, Kans.: State Printing Works, 1874), p. 134; C. Henry Smith, *Christian Peace: Four Hundred Years of Mennonite Peace Principles and Practice* (Peace Committee of the General Conference of the Mennonite Church of North America, 1938), p. 21; C. Henry Smith, *The Coming of the Russian Mennonites: An Episode in the Settling of the Last Frontier, 1874-1884*, (Berne, Ind.: Mennonite Book Concern, 1927), p. 266; David C. Wedel, *The Story of Alexanderwohl, 1874-1974* (Goessel, Kans.: Goessel Centennial Committee, 1974), p. 27.

48. Gene Sharp, *The Politics of Nonviolent Action* (Boston, Mass.: Porter Sargent Publishing, 1973), p. 242.

49. Peter Brock, *Pacifism in Europe to 1914, op. cit.*, p. 439, C. J.

Dyck, *An Introduction to Mennonite History* (Scottdale, Pa.: Herald Press, 1967), pp. 140-1; and esp. John B. Toews, *op. cit.*, pp. 15-40.

50. Sanford Calvin Yoder, *For Conscience Sake: A Study of Mennonite Migrations Resulting from the World War*, (Scottdale, Pa.: Herald Press, 1945), p. 47.

51. Keith L. Sprunger, James C. Juhnke, and John D. Waltner, *Voices Against War: A Guide to the Schowalter Oral History Collection on World War I Conscientious Objection*, (North Newton, Kans.: Bethel College, 1973), page 2 from the Introductory Forward by James Juhnke. See also Ray H. Abrams, *Preachers present Arms* (Scottdale, Pa,: Herald Press, 1933, 1969), pp. 77-92, 188.

52. Margaret Entz, "War Bond Drives and the Kansas Mennonite Response," *Mennonite Life* (September, 1975), p. 9. This six-page article is a comprehensive treatment of the Liberty Loan campaigns during World War I and of their impact on Mennonite life. It won the Bethel College Mennonite Contributions contest in 1975.

53. James C. Juhnke, "John Schrag Espionage Case," *Mennonite Life* (July, 1967), pp. 121-2. Charles Gordon's testimony concerning the persecution of John Schrag appears on pages 20-21 of *Mennonite Life* (September, 1975). Additional information is to be found in James C. Juhnke's *A People of Two Kingdoms: The Political Acculturation of the Kansas Mennonites* (North Newton, Kans.: Faith and Life Press, 1975), p. 104, and in Donald E. Durnbaugh's *The Believers' Church* (New York: The Macmillan Company, 1968), p. 258.

54. Elizabeth Hershberger Bauman, *Coals of Fire* (Scottdale, Pa.: Herald Press, 1954), p. 37.

55. John A. Hostetler, *op. cit.*, pp. 130 and 197; C. Henry Smith, *The Coming of the Russian Mennonites, op. cit.*, pp. 292-3, 276-82; Cornelius J. Dyck, *op. cit.*, pp. 236-7 (section on "The Hutterites"); and Ray H. Abrams, *op. cit.*, p. 188.

56. James Russell Lowell (1819-1891) in his poem, "The Present Crisis." Included in *The Brethren Hymnal* (Elgin, Ill.: Brethren Publishing House, 1951), Hymn 569.

57. Rufus D. Bowman, *The Church of the Brethren and War* (Elgin, Ill.: Brethren Press, 1944), pp. 238 ff; Dale W. Brown, *Brethren and Pacifism* (Elgin, Ill.: Brethren Press, 1970), p. 47.

58. Austin Regier, "Christianity and Conscription as Viewed by a Non-Registrant," *The Mennonite* (November 30, 1948), pp. 13-15, and "The Faith of a Convict," *The Mennonite* (Feb. 15, 1949) pp. 8-10.

59. Quoted in a War Resisters League leaflet; Nat Hentoff, *Peace Agitator: The Story of A. J. Muste* (New York: The Macmillan Company, 1963), esp. pp. 125-9; editorial on "A. J. Muste," *Fellowship* (March, 1967), p. 3.

60. Robert Calvert, *op. cit.*, p. xiii; Lillian Schlissel, *op cit.*, pp 398 ff; *Handbook on Nonpayment of War Taxes* (Cincinnati, Ohio: Peacemaker Movement, 1963, 1966, 1967, 1968, 1971), 50 pages. Current address of *The Peacemaker* Magazine is: Box 4793, Arcata, Calif. 95521.

61. Marion Bromley, "No Reason to Fear," *Friends Journal* (February 15, 1976), pp. 106-107.

62. Wendy Schwartz, "Tax Resistance and WRL," *WRL News* (July-August 1974), pp. 5-6.

63. "They Would Not Fight" flyer and a personal letter from Bob Seeley of CCCO dated April 14, 1978, 2 pages. The address of CCCO is: 2016 Walnut Street, Philadelphia, Pa. 19103.

64. Thomas C. Cornell and James H. Forest (editors), *A Penny a Copy: Readings from the Catholic Worker* (New York: The Macmillan Co., 1968), pp. 52-3.

65. *Sojourners* (March, 1977), p. 23; Jim Forest and Wes Michaelson, "Encountering Dorothy Day," *Sojourners* (Dec., 1976), pp. 12-19; Joan Thomas, *The Years of Grief and Laughter* (Phoenix, Arizona. Hennacy Press, 1974), 342 pages.

66. "A Plea for the Support of the War Tax Objector" (October, 1971), 7 pages; Bernard Survil, "War: Individual Witness or Corporate Response," p. 2.

67. *The Catholic Worker* (October-November, 1977), p. 5. Mailing address is: 36 East First St., New York, NY 10003. See special issue on "The Burden of the Berrigans," *Holy Cross Quarterly*, Vol. 4, No. 1, (January, 1971), 80 pages.

68. Delton Franz, "Military Related Income Taxes," *The Washington Memo*, Vol. X, No. 2 (March-April, 1978), pp. 1-3.

69. The following is only a partial list of war tax statements:

"A Call to Action" by members of the Mennonite and Brethren in Christ Church of North America (Minneapolis, Nov. 21, 1970);

"A Statement of the Church of the Brethren on War" (1451 Dundee Avenue, Elgin, Ill.: The Brethren Press), four pages; also

"Obedience to God and Civil Disobedience," four pages.

"Covenant-Statement of War Tax Workshop Participants," Western District Conference Seminar, North Newton, Kans. (Feb. 27, 1971).

"The Way of Peace," A Christian Declaration Adopted by the General Conference Mennonite Church, at Fresno, Calif., August 19, 1971 (Newton, Kans.: Faith and Life Press, 1972), 24 pages.

"Statement Concerning the World Peace Tax Fund" adopted by the Bethel College Mennonite Church, North Newton, Kans.: on June 1, 1975 (*God and Caesar* newsletter, June, 1975, p. 5).

"General Conference War Tax Resolution #33" adopted at St.

Catharines, Ontario, during August 1974 (*God and Caesar* newsletter, January 1975, p. 2).

"A Position Paper on War Taxes" prepared by a task force of the Bethel College Mennonite Church, North Newton, Kans. 67117 (April 3, 1977), 9 pages.

"Waubee Peace Pledge I & II," prepared by participants of a war tax retreat held at Camp Mack, Ind. (November 4-6, 1977).

70. *The Way of Peace, op. cit.*, p. 18; J. Howard Kauffman and Leland Harder, *Anabaptists Four Centuries Later* (Scottdale, Pa. and Kitchener, Ont.: Herald Press, 1975), p. 134.

71. Address: *God and Caesar*, Box 347, Newton, Kans. 67114.

72. "Tax Resistance Group in Japan Gains Support," *The Mennonite* (February 18, 1975), p. 103. "Cites War Tax Resistance in Japan," *Mennonite Weekly Review* (August 31, 1978) p. 6; Michio Ohno, "A Short Study on War Tax Resistance in Japan" (mimeographed article). Address is: Conscientious Objection to Military Tax (COMIT), 2-35-18 Asahigaoka, Hino City, Tokyo 191, Japan. They publish *The Plowshare* with a one-page English summary (overseas subscription, $4).

73. Ruth C. Stoltzfus, "War Tax Research Report: Challenging Withholding Law on First Amendment Grounds," a special study prepared for CHM, General Conference Mennonite Church, Newton, Kans., August, 1975, consisting of 16 pages.

74. J. R. Burkholder, "Radical Pacifism Challenges the Mennonite Church," (paper prepared for the Mennonite Theological Study Group, January 1960), p. 2.

75. Estimated in Fiscal 1977 budget by War Resisters' League, 339 Lafayette St., New York, N.Y. 10012. Canadian readers who may want to trace Canada's development as a manufacturer and merchandiser of war materials, should consult Ernie Regehr's *Making A Killing* (Toronto, Canada: McClelland and Stewart Limited, 1975), 135 pages.

76. For supplementary information see Kaufman, *What Belongs to Caesar? op. cit.*, pp. 64-70; Stuart Chase, *Where's the Money Coming From?* (New York: The Twentieth Century Fund, 1943), 179 pages.

77. *Congressional Record* (February 23, 1966). See also *Churches and Phone Tax Resistance* (122 West Franklin Ave., Minneapolis, Minn.: Minnesota Clergy and Laymen Concerned, 1970).

78. *Ibid*; Diogenes, *The April Game: Secrets of an Internal Revenue Agent* (Chicago, Ill.: Playboy Press, 1973), pp. 52 ff; Lillian Doris (ed), *The American Way in Taxation: Internal Revenue, 1862-1963* (Englewood Cliffs, N.J.: Prentice-Hall, Inc. 1963), 301 pages.

79. Excerpt from the MCC Peace Section, *Washington Memo* (Nov.-Dec., 1973), p. 6.

80. Phil M. Shenk, "World Peace Tax Fund," *The Mennonite* (December 13, 1977), p. 735. (Current address for WPTF's National Office is 2111 Florida Ave., N.W., Washington, D.C. 20008.

81. Telephone tax protest card circulated by Minnesota Clergy and Laity Concerned.

82. Personal conversation on April 21, 1978.

83. Levi O. Keidel, "The Mennonite Credibility Gap," *The Mennonite* (December 23, 1975), p. 731.

84. "Make Gifts Instead of Paying Tax," *Mennonite Weekly Review* (March 22, 1973), p. 6; Linda Schmidt, " 'War Tax' Refusers Persisting," *Mennonite Weekly Review* (August 24, 1978), p. 5.

85. Cornelia Lehn, "My Pilgrimage with War Tax Resistance," *God and Caesar* (June, 1976), p.2.

86. From a leaflet revised in March, 1974.

87. Ivan Friesen, "Letter to the Editor," *God and Caesar* (October, 1975), pp. 4-5.

88. Robert Calvert, *op. cit.*, pp. 58-59; James R. Klassen, "Letters to the IRS," *God and Caesar* (June and July, 1978 issues), pp. 8-10 and pp. 14-15 respectively.

89. Kaufman, *op. cit.*, p. 81; "Baez Files Claim with IRS for Refund of 1965 Tax," *Fellowship Peace Information Edition* (October, 1966), p. 2.

90. Ammon Hennacy, *op. cit.*, p. 334.

91. Quoted by Phil M. Shenk, *op. cit.*, p. 735.

92. Melvin D. Schmidt, *op. cit.*, pp. 240-241.

93. Janet Reedy, "Our Day in Court," *God and Caesar* (June, 1977), pp. 3-6; Jack Cady, "An Open Letter," *Friends Journal* (February 15, 1976) pp. 102-105.

94. John A. Lapp, "Tax Deductions and the Nationalizing of the Churches," *MCC Peace Section Newsletter* (April 15, 1972), p. 1.

95. *Sojourners* (March, 1977), p. 23. Originally printed ·in the April, 1960, issue of *Liberation* under the title, "Not So Long Ago: My Affair with the Internal Revenue Bureau," pp. 17-19.

96. Nat Hentoff, *op. cit.*, p. 129.

97. Personal letter to author dated April 17, 1978, and a letter which was printed in both *The Peacemaker* (September 2, 1977) and *God and Caesar* (November, 1977), pp. 6-7. Also see Edmund Wilson, *The Cold War and the Income Tax: A Protest* (New York: Farrar, Straus and Company, 1963), pp. 105-107.

98. Dave Wood, *et. al.*, Letter from Minnesota War Tax Resistance and Alternative Fund, 122 W. Franklin, Room 302, Minneapolis, Minn. 55404, dated March 20, 1978.

99. Gordon C. Zahn, Review of *In Solitary Witness: The Life and*

Death of Franz Jägerstätter appearing in *Fellowship* (March, 1965).

100. Kenneth D. Eberhard, *The Alienated Christain: Theology of Alienation* (Philadelphia, Pa.: Pilgrim Press, 1971), p. 133. The book is now available in softbound edition (278 pages) from The Liturgical Press, Collegeville, Minn., 56321.

101. Christopher Fry, *A Sleep of Prisoners* (a play) (New York and London: Oxford University Press, 1951), pp. 47-8.

102. Howard E. Royer, "Portraits of Asia," *Messenger* (February 15, 1971), p. 31. (A people-to-people peace treaty undertaking of the National Student Association by Doug Hostetter in Vietnam, December, 1970.)

103. Walter Klaassen, *Anabaptism: Neither Catholic nor Protestant, op. cit.*, p. 81.

104. Margaret E. Hirst, *op. cit.* p. 347, or P. Mayer, *The Pacifist Conscience* (New York: Holt, Rinehart and Winston, 1966), p. 97.

105. Donald D. Kaufman, "Paying for war while praying for peace: dilemma of individuals and the body," *Sojourners* (March, 1977), p. 17.

106. John M. Drescher, *op. cit.*, p.545.

107. Melvin D. Schmidt, *op. cit.*, p. 245.

108. Marlin Jeschke, "Render to Caesar or to God?" (Revision of a presentation made to the Peace Assembly in Chicago, Illinois, during November 16-18, 1972; revised on March 20, 1973), p. 3.

109. Willard Swartley, "The Christian and Payment of War Taxes" (Mimeographed study presented to the Mennonite War Tax Conference held at Kitchener, Ontario, on November 1, 1975), p. 10.

110. James W. Douglass, *The Non-Violent Cross: A Theology of Revolution and Peace* (London: The Macmillan Company, 1966, 1968), p. 213; see also Charlie Lord, *The Rule of the Sword* (Newton, Kans.: Faith and Life Press, 1978), 68 pages.

111. Marlin Jeschke, *op.cit.*, p. 3.

112. Jean Lasserre, *War and the Gospel* (Scottdale, Pa.: Herald Press, 1962), p. 92. The Apostle Peter in Acts 4:19 and 5:29.

113. Martin Buber, Will Herberg (editor), *The Writings of Martin Buber* (New York: New American Library, 1958), p. 28.

114. Pope Leo XIII quoted by Ammon Hennacy, *The Book of Ammon* (P.O. Box 655, Salt Lake City, Utah, 1965), p. 298.

115. Arthur G. Gish, *The New Left and Christian Radicalism* (Grand Rapids, Mich.: Wm. B. Eerdmans, 1970), p. 70, and William Wiswedel, "The Handbüchlein of 1558," *Mennonite Quarterly Review*, XXIX (July, 1955), pp. 213-214.

116. Personal letter from Bill Samuel, September 16, 1976, p. 1.

117. Poem by Jessica Powers entitled "The Little Nation."

APPENDIX A

The Harassed Taxpayer's Prayer
Consider the humor of Art Buchwald who wrote the following prayer as spoken by the harassed taxpayer:

"Heavenly Father, we beseech you in our hour of need to look down kindly on your humble taxpaying servants who have given all we possess to the almighty Internal Revenue Service. Grant us that we have completed our Form 1040 correctly so no power will find fault with it. We pray to God that we have added lines 12, 13, 14, and 15 accurately, and that we have subtracted line 17 from line 16 so our adjusted gross income is computed to their divine satisfaction.

"We ask you, O Lord, to protect our exemptions and bless our deductions as outlined in Schedule A (Form 1040) (see Chapters 10 and 11). Have mercy on those of us who failed to wisely estimate our payments during the year, and must now borrow from Peter to pay Paul. Blessed are they who spent more than they earned and contributed so much to the economy.

"Give us strength, Lord, so that we may dwell in a lower tax bracket forever and ever (as outlined in Publication 17, the Revised 1972 Edition). Yea though we walk through the valley of the shadow of bankruptcy (see tax rate schedule X, Y, Z, or if applicable Schedule D or schedule G or maximum tax form 4726) there is no one to comfort us."

—Reprinted by permission of Art Buchwald.

APPENDIX B

The Waubee Peace Pledges
The peace pledges on page 86 grew out of a war tax retreat held at Camp Mack in Indiana, November 4-6, 1977.

Jesus Christ is Lord and we pledge our lives to His lordship. This is a pledge which we do make and we can make because the Lord fills His people with faith, hope, and love. This is a pledge which we make with humility, but also with conviction, aware of the risks, since under all circumstances, we must obey God rather than people.

We believe in the resurrection of Jesus Christ, knowing that it is in the resurrection that we have our life. We need follow death no more. Death is conquered. God chooses life for us.

We therefore pledge ourselves to the service of life and the renunciation of death. Jesus is the way and the truth and His way is the way of peace. We will seek to follow in that way of peace . . . and we will seek to oppose the way of war.

Specifically we make this pledge to our brothers and sisters in Christ:

1. Since we do not give our bodies for war, neither will we give our money. We will refuse payment of federal telephone taxes and federal income taxes which go for military purposes. Where our treasure is, there our hearts will be also. If our treasure is involved in making war, and if that means legal or other jeopardy for any of us, we will seek to support one another as sisters and brothers. The earth is the Lord's and the fullness thereof. Render unto God what belongs to God.

2. We further pledge ourselves to urgently communicate with brothers and sisters in our churches, urging them to join us in refusing money for war. We will also work to have annual meetings of our churches take a firm stand against payment of war taxes and to have our church agencies agree to refuse withholding of these taxes from the pay of employees. We believe that we who are the body of Christ should not serve as a military tax collection agency.

3. We further pledge ourselves to keep our hearts and lives open to the movement of God's Spirit and to follow where Jesus might lead us on the path of peace. We pray for help and guidance—that we might be instruments of God's peace.

Because we are at different points of commitment, a second pledge came out of this conference. There was a common understanding by participants in the conference that Jesus is the King of Peace and that it is wrong to pay taxes for war, but for some that witness to life takes a different form.

Waubee Peace Pledge II

We, in spirit and in conscience, affirm the Waubee Peace Pledge and fully support our sisters and brothers of that covenant. At this time in our lives we feel unable to commit ourselves to nonpayment of income and phone taxes. We do commit our time, energy, and resources to searching for alternate channels of resistance, and pledge ourselves to continual seeking of God's will for us in acting definitively to oppose those taxes for payment of war.

We give thanks for the freedom given us through Christ which enables us in this search and we pray for the strength and hope to use our freedom as servants of God.

APPENDIX C

A Parable

Once, in a certain land, there were peasant villages on which napalm bombs fell; mines exploded along the paths and in the fields. Many of the villagers and their children were hurt and many killed.

When it became known that the villagers were suffering, many Christians wondered who was responsible.

A Quaker of good repute thought Congress was responsible and supported efforts to lobby the legislature to cut off funding for such bloodshed. He himself continued to give money to Congress each year on April 15 because the law said it was required.

A Catholic woman, daily communicant, thought upon the slaughter of innoncent children and decided to pray each day for peace. She did not think about paying for the bombs and mines because that money was automatically taken out of her pay each week and sent to the government by her employer.

A Mennonite was troubled in conscience because he knew his taxes were paying for bombs and mines. Thinking about the future, he gave vigorous support to the World Peace Tax Fund which would provide by law that he could elect for reasons of conscience that his taxes be used only for non-military projects. He looked forward in faith to the day when this law would provide solace for his conscience.

A Baptist minister thought that the president was responsible and urged people to vote for a canditate who promised peace. Many in his congregation worked for companies making weapons; others were in the military; all were good, law-abiding citizens. The minister gave thanks to be shepherd of such a fine flock.

An elder in an Hutterian community thought upon the evils of war and recommended a relief effort to care for the families and the injured. He said, "If we knew our taxes were going only for war, of course, we would not pay them. But what can we do? Some of our taxes go for good purposes too, like schools and roads. Besides, our religious life might be disrupted if we were not faithful to the government and obedient to its laws."

Now a young man, an atheist, his eyes and heart open to suffering, made a decision to refuse to pay for war. And when the war against the villages was over and the government increased the military budget by $4 billion and continued to build nuclear weapons, he also refused to pay for this.

Which of these was neighbor to the villagers?

—By John Schuchardt. Reprinted by permission from *God and Caesar*, November, 1977.

APPENDIX D

A War Tax Protester's Letter to the Editor
I have recently received threatening letters from a terrorist group which asks that I contribute money for construction of

dangerous weapons. This group makes certain claims which in the past led me to send thousands of dollars to pay for its militaristic programs. The group claimed:

1. It was concerned with peace and freedom.
2. It would provide protection for me and my family.
3. It was my duty to make these payments, and
4. I was free from personal responsibility for how this money was spent in individual cases.

Last year, for the first time, I realized that these claims were fradulent and I refused to make further payments. Although there were threats of "penalties" I am happy to report that no more serious extortion efforts have been made.

However, again this year I have been solicited to send money. In the meantime, I have ascertained that the organization which calls itself the United States of America, already has in its possession 423 B-52 and 73 FB-111 bombers with 3,800 nuclear warheads, 1,000 Minutemen missiles each with 10 megaton warheads (500 Hiroshima bombs), 54 Titan missiles with 1.5 megaton warheads or three individually targeted warheads of 160 kilotons each, 41 ballistic missiles, submarines each carrying 10 missiles with MIRVed warheads.

This group has felt the interests of peace could be served by sending 13 nuclear bombs to Israel and by selling $13 billion of the most devastating weapons to countries around the world last year. Bribery is used to promote these sales. Support is given to fascist governments rather than to democratic ones. In fact, although the entire year of 1976 was spent celebrating the American revolution, it seems that any person associated with revolution or freedom or peace today is automatically condemned. I write this letter from jail for speaking and acting for peace at the Pentagon.

May those who love their country, love their people and all people, be warned not to support this group. Its leaders talk of "first strike," "limited nuclear war," "counterforce," and "MAD"—mutual assured destruction. Can that be sanity? The cry of Wolf! Wolf! (or is it Bear! Bear!) is again being made to frighten us to pay $92 billion for 244 B-1 bombers, and to build 30 Trident submarines (the first is under construction and will carry 24 missiles, each with 17 MARV warheads. That's 408

89

targets, 2000 Nagasakis, three times the explosive force dropped by the United States in World War II, Korea, and Vietnam. (Remember Vietnam was 8 million tons, four times the tonnage of all of World War II). All under the command of one man.

Dear friends, I hope you may be alerted not to support this terrorist organization. They depend on your cooperation and money and usually try to collect it on April 15. They now possess a total of 30,000 nuclear bombs and each day manufacture three more at Amarillo, Texas.

Peace is not brought by bombs but by a spirit of repentance, forgiveness, and love for enemies. Let us seek a future for our children. Time is short. In eight years, 35 nations will have these weapons of terror, each one able to vaporize a city in an instant. No matter where you live, you are sitting on ground zero right now. AWAKE!

—By *John Schuchardt,* used by permission.

APPENDIX E

Unity

Refrain:
Jesus, help us live in peace.
From our blindness set us free.
Fill us with Your healing love.
Help us live in unity.

Many times we disagree
O'er what's right or wrong to do.
It's so hard to really see
From the other's point of view.
(Repeat the refrain.)

How we long for pow'r and fame.
Seeking ev'ry earthly thing.
We forget the One who came
As a servant, not a king.
(Repeat the refrain.)

—Reprinted by permission of the author, *Jerry Derstine.*

APPENDIX F

We Didn't Know
(James 1:22-25)

Chorus:
> We didn't know at all,
> We didn't see a thing,
> You can't hold us to blame,
> What could we do?
> It was a terrible shame,
> But we can't bear the blame,
> Oh no, not us, we didn't know.

1. We didn't know said the burgomeister
   About those camps at the edge of town.
   It was Hitler and his crew that tore the German nation down,
   We saw the cattle cars it's true and maybe they carried a Jew or two,
   Woke us up as they rumbled through
   But what did you expect me to do?

2. We didn't know said the congregation,
   Singing a hymn in a church of white.
   Press was full of lies about us
   Preacher told us we were right.
   Outside agitators came and they burned some churches and they put the blame
   Using southern people's names to set our colored folks aflame.
   Maybe some of our boys got hot
   And a couple of niggers and reds got shot.
   They should've stayed where they belonged—
   The preacher would've told us if we done wrong.

3. We didn't know said the puzzled voter,
   Watching the president on TV.

91

Guess we gotta drop those bombs if we're gonna keep South
  Asia free.
President's such a peaceful man,
I'm sure he's got some kind of plan.
Say we're torturing prisoners of war but I can't believe that
  stuff no more,
Torturing prisoners is a communist game—
And you can bet they're doing the same.
Wish this war was over and through but what do you expect
  me to do?

—Reprinted from the Koinonia record album, "Friends."

APPENDIX G

My People, I Am Your Security

Several weeks prior to the 10th Assembly of the Mennonite
World Conference in Wichita, Kansas, in July, 1978, David H.
Janzen of Newton, Kansas, received a letter from Ladon Sheats
who is in prison for his Christian witness against the arms race.
Ladon expressed the hope that the Mennonite World
Conference would be called to confront the world-wide arma-
ments build-up.

As David fasted and prayed over this letter, the Lord spoke
the following message to him. He trembled as he wrote,
wondering what temptations or persecutions this prophecy
might bring on him. But the Lord assured him that if he
obeyed one step at a time, he could trust God with the future.
So he shared the prophecy with his congregation, the New
Creation Fellowship. The congregation confirmed it.

The statement was then presented to the Nuclear Disarmament Group of about seventy-five persons at World
Conference. They in turn arranged to have it read to the entire
assembly, urging people to respond as the Spirit of Christ
would lead them.

My people, proclaim to your governments and your neighbors that you do not need armaments for your security.

> I am your security. I will give the peacemakers glory as I defended and glorified my own defenseless Son, Jesus.

My kingdom is international.

> I am pleased that my children gather all around the globe to give allegience to One Kingdom. My kingdom is coming in power. No powers, not even the powers of nuclear warfare can destroy my kingdom.
>
> My kingdom is from beyond this earth.
>
> The world thought it had killed Jesus, Jesus through whom I have overcome the world. Therefore, Be Not Afraid.

You are a gathering of my kingdom;

> My kingdom will last forever.
>
> Taste the first fruits now;
>
> Embrace the international fellowship in Christ and praise Me Together.

Do not fear the nuclear holocaust.

> Do not panic or take unloving short-cuts to fight the armaments monster.
>
> I go before you to do battle.

This is a spiritual battle, the battle to destroy war.

> Do not attempt to fight this battle on your own.
>
> Fear, guilt and anger will make you spiritual prisoners of the Enemy if you fight on your own authority.
>
> Learn to hear my voice. Learn to be at unity with those who love Me.
>
> I will lead and protect My army.
>
> I will co-ordinate the battle in many nations.

I want to show you where the idols of this age are hidden.

> Learn where are the missile silos, the bomb factories, the centers of military command, the prisons for dissenters.
>
> Understand that those who bow down to Fear trust in these idols for salvation.
>
> Stand beside their idols and proclaim My liberating kingdom. Invite them to share your life in Me. Perfect love must be your weapon, for perfect love casts out Fear.

If you obey My call, you will be persecuted, misunderstood, powerless.
You will share in my suffering for the world,
But I will never abandon you. You belong to my international,
eternal kingdom.

Do not say time is running out. Do not threaten or despair.
I am the Lord of time. There is no time to seek the world's ap-
proval,
But there is time to do what I will lay before you.

By my mercy I have extended time.
I extended time for a perverse human race when I called Noah.
I lengthened the time of repentance by sending my prophets.
I have averted nuclear disaster many times for you.
Jesus offers you all time, time to repent and come to Me.
Obey my call and there will be time to do what I am laying
before you.
Now is the time.

I want you to learn who around the world has refused to bow down to
the god of fear or worship weapons of terror.
Hold hands around the world with My soldiers, My prisoners.
Pray for each other and share My strength with them.
I love those who put their trust in Me and will put joy in their
hearts.

There is time to build My kingdom.
There is time to protest armaments and to build a spiritual com-
munity for those who turn from the idols of fear.
Call them to join you in the security that flows from Father, Son
and Spirit,
My community, given for you.

My seed is planted in every one of my children;
It is waiting to break the husks of fear that it may grow toward
My Son's light.
I did not plant my spirit in Russians, or Americans, Arabs or Is-
raelis, Capitalists or Communists. . . . . that they might
destroy each other,
But that they might recognize my image in each other and come
together in praise of their creator's name.

94

My beloved children,
> Share the burden of my heart,
> Know my love so that you may learn to die for one another.
> There is time to do this.
> Trust me and I will sustain you within my kingdom forever.

—David H. Janzen

APPENDIX H

Helpful Organizations

American Friends Service Committee
160 N. 15th Street
Philadelphia, PA 19102

Brethren Service Commission
Church of the Brethren,
1451 Dundee Ave.,
Elgin, IL 60120

Catholic Worker
36 E. First Street
New York, NY 10003

Center on Law and Pacifism
300 West Apsley Street
Philadelphia, PA 19144

Central Committee for Conscientious Objectors
2016 Walnut Street
Philadelphia, PA 19103

Coalition for a New Foreign and Military Policy
120 Maryland Ave. NE
Washington, DC 20002

Conscientious Objection to Military Tax (COMIT)
2-35-18 Asahigaoka
Hino City, Tokyo 191, Japan

Fellowship of Reconciliation
Box 271
Nyack, NY 10960

Friends Committee on National Legislation
104 C. Street, N.E.
Washington, DC 20002

God and Caesar
Box 347
Newton, KS 67114

Minnesota War Tax Resistance & Alternative Fund
122 West Franklin, Room 302
Minneapolis, MN 55404

National Council for a World Peace Tax Fund
2111 Florida Ave., N.W.
Washington, DC 20008

National Interreligious Service Board
550 Washington Building
15th Street and New York Avenue, N.W.
Washington, DC 20005

Peace Pledge Union
Dick Sheppard House
6 Endsleigh Street
London, England WC1H ODX

Peacemakers
P.O. Box 627
Garberville, CA 95440

Peace Section
Mennonite Central Committee
Akron, PA 17501

Promoting Enduring Peace, Inc.
Box 103
Woodmont, CT 06460

SANE
318 Massachusetts Ave., N.E.
Washington, DC 20002

Taxation with Representation
Suite 204, 1523 L. Street, N.W.
Washington, DC 20005

Taxpayers Against War
P.O. Box 15394
San Francisco, CA 94115

War Resisters' League & War Tax Resistance
339 Lafayette Street
New York, NY 10012

The Washington Memo
Mennonite Central Committee
100 Maryland Ave., N.E.
Washington, DC 20002

Women's International League for Peace & Freedom
1213 Race Street
Philadelphia, PA 19107

Year One Newsletter
c/o Jonah House
1933 Park Avenue
Baltimore, MD 21217

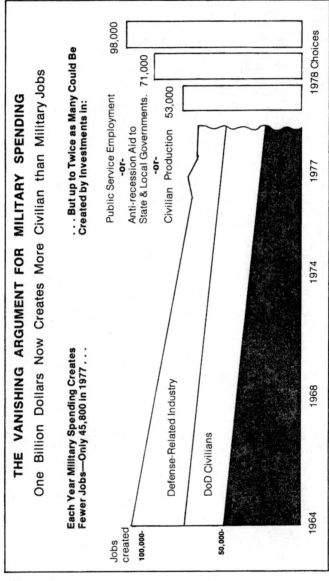

THE VANISHING ARGUMENT FOR MILITARY SPENDING

One Billion Dollars Now Creates More Civilian than Military Jobs

Each Year Military Spending Creates Fewer Jobs—Only 45,800 in 1977 . . . .

. . . But up to Twice as Many Could Be Created by Investments in:

Public Service Employment   98,000
-or-
Anti-recession Aid to
State & Local Governments.   71,000
-or-
Civilian Production   53,000

1978 Choices

Jobs created
100,000-
50,000-

Defense-Related Industry

DoD Civilians

1964   1968   1974   1977

Source: Center for Defense Information. Based on data from Department of Defense, Congressional Budget Office, and Bureau of Labor Statistics.

APPENDIX I

The Vanishing Argument for Military Spending

Ironically, the usual justification for labor support of the Pentagon—that military spending is good for the economy—runs contrary to a growing body of evidence. The war economy turns out to be a very poor bargain. Far from helping the economy, military spending actually contributes to unemployment, worsens inflation, and depletes the heart of the industrial economy. By diverting an excessive portion of our national wealth to the military, the nation has been spending itself into a permanent economic crisis.

Consider the following: Defense spending is one of the least efficient means of creating jobs. Almost any private or public alternative will yield more jobs per dollar than arms production. As the defense sector has become more technological, the level of overall employment has decreased. In California, for example, defense spending is currently at an all-time high, but total aerospace employment has dropped from a 1968 high of 750,000 to approximately 440,000 today.

—U.S. Senator *George McGovern* in a March, 1978, letter to constituents.

APPENDIX J

Audiovisual Resources

"Conscience and War Taxes" (Turning War Taxes into Dollars for Peace)—(20-min. 79 slide presentation with soundtrack on cassette tape.) Produced in 1978, this slide set recognizes that it is with our tax dollars that we shape the world in which we live. Because arms spending is by definition the most inflationary of all expenditures, it traces the history of the U.S. income tax, examines some of the economic consequences of military spending, and discusses a legal alternative which could provide dollars for peace instead of war. A remarkable portrayal of the responsibility of government to recognize the right of conscience on the issue of military taxes. A useful tool for educating and organizing ourselves for a more responsive tax system. Purchase price: $50 each, rental; $15 a week. Available from the National Council for a World Peace Tax Fund, 2111 Florida Ave., N.W., Washington, DC 20008-1923. Tel. (202) 483-3751; Email: info@peacetaxfund.org.

An Act of Conscience, 1997, 90 minutes, color, 35mm. Narrated by Martin Sheen. This is a personal and profound film that depicts the significance and devolution of a life of long moral and political commitment. It tells the story of war tax resisters Randy Kehler and Betsy Corner of Colrain, MA over a five-year period. The couple nonviolently resisted the seizure of their home with the support of hundreds of community activists in an encampment. The government auctioned off their home—an extraordinary story of working class efforts to resist war and military spending. Filmmaker Robbie Leppzer, Turning Tide Productions (in association with Cinemax Reel Life), POB 864, Wendell, MA 01379, Tel.: (508) 544-8313, FAX (508) 544-7989.

A Force More Powerful, Ackerman, Peter. Christopher Kruegler and Jack Homer. Two videotapes total length 3 hours. Available from Video Finders, 4401 Sunset Blvd., Los Angeles, CA 90027. $39.95 (for both tapes) + $6.95 shipping & handling.

Blood Makes the Grass Grow, 1997, 46 minutes. This video features the stories of Gulf War conscientious objectors. Available from MCC: (717) 859-1151, or MCCResources@mcc.org

Change of Command, video with study guide features the stories and faith journeys of six military veterans whose inner voice clashed with their military duties. Available for free loan from any MCC office.

Compelled by Conscience: Why We Need a Peace Tax Fund, 2001, 15 minutes, DVD or VHS. A documentary presenting background leading to the development of Peace Tax Fund legislation in the U.S., including footage of the hearing before a Subcommittee on Select Revenue Measures, May 21, 1992. Available from the NCPTF office for $12. www. peacetaxfund.org

The CPS Story: Oral History of Mennonites in WW II, VHS, 30 minutes. Narrated by Roger Juhnke, Bethel College Schowalter Oral History Project, North Newton, Kansas 67117. Voices include H.A. Fast, Loris Habegger, Harley Stucky, and Esko Loewen.

The Good War and Those Who Refused to Fight It, 60 minutes. Documentary film about conscientious objectors during World War II. Independent Television Service presents a film produced, directed, and written by Judith Ehrlich and Rich Tejada-Flores. Photographed by Vicente Franco. Edited by Ken Schneider. Music by Barney Jones. Associate Producer and Archival Research by Laurie Coyle. Narrated by Edward Asner. Although the Selective Service law of 1940 promised COs work of national importance, many found themselves in near slave labor conditions. Viewers will find it an expanding companion to the six-part documentary series from PBS called *A Force More Powerful: A Century of Nonviolent Conflict, 3 hours*. Two videotapes available from Video Finders, 4401 Sunset Blvd., Los Angeles, CA 90027.

Guns or Butter? Uncle Sam's Military Tapeworm, 30-minute slide set with cassette tape narration. Exposes the growth of U.S. military spending since 1945; portrays the draining of resources needed for civilian programs at home and abroad. Narrated by Paul Newman. Produced by and available from SANE (A Citizen's Organization for a Sane World).

Hidden in Plain Sight, 60 minutes. Documentary about the School of the Americas (SOA) in Fort Benning, GA which does combat training for Latin American soldiers. Shows Roy Bourgeois and citizens demonstrating annually to close this dubious program which destroys lives and families in the Southern Hemisphere.

Hiroshima-Nagasaki, August, 1945, 16 minutes, b/w. A short film edited from three hours of footage shot by Japanese photographers just after the holocaust killed 200,000 citizens. For 25 years the U.S. military suppressed the footage until Japanese pressure forced its release to the world. This is a very gruesome and sobering film about nuclear annihilation. Not for children below high school age. Available from Peace and Justice Support Network, Mennonite Church USA, P.O. Box 370, Elkhart, IN 46515. Website: http://peace.mennolink.org

The Magician, 13 minutes, b/w. A simple allegory about war. The children are out for play when they chance upon the 'magician.' He entices them into his shooting gallery where he teaches them to shoot first at targets, then at dolls, then . . . There is only one word in this powerful story, and yet the charade of war is unmasked. Demonstrates how the military mesmerizes young people. Available from the American Friends Service Committee, 4211 Grand Ave., Des Moines, IA 50312.

Military Tax Resistance: Claiming Our Human Right Not to Kill, 80 minute audio CD broadcast live on KFAI radio's Wave Project on Sunday, 2002-03-24. KFAI host Don Olson interviews John Harmon and Charles Johnson. A project of Friends for a Non-violent World, 1150 Selby Ave., Saint Paul, MN 55104-6534. www.FNVW.org

More than a Paycheck: War Tax Resistance in America, 1985, 138 slides and tape, 20 minutes. A good introduction to war tax resistance. Covers motivations, history, methods, and consequences. Rental $25, purchase $75. Obtain from NWTRCC, P.O. Box 150533, Brooklyn, NY 11215. Tel. (800) 269-7464.

Parable, 22 minutes, color. A short, provocative film where no word is spoken—but you have to be spiritually deaf to miss the message. In the Gospels Jesus teaches us by using parables. Today a parable might begin like this: "Once there was a great circus, and in the march of nations and peoples, a great circus parade in which some were participants, some merely spectators. A parade in which human beings seldom knew one another or cared for one another; and into this great circus of life came a man—who dared to be different." Available for purchase or rental through CINE-CATH, Catholic Missions, 371 5th St., Manistee, MI 49660.

Paying for Peace: War Tax Resistance in the United States, 1993, 30 minutes, VHS. An award-winning documentary featuring interviews with Ernst and Marion Bromley, Maurice McCrackin, Wally and Juanita Nelson, Brian Wilson, and others. Available from producer Carol Coney, 4002 Hwy, 78 Suite 530-142, Snellville, GA 30039. Email: ckconey@catgoddess.com.

The Race Nobody Wins, 15 minutes, color slide/filmstrip with guide and cassette tape. An inexpensive resource on the costliness of the international arms race, particularly the threat of nuclear war. Utilizes clear graphics. Narrated by Tony Randall. Rent or purchase from SANE, 318 Massachusetts Ave., NE, Washington, DC 20002.

SOA: Guns and Greed, 20-minute video. A broad introduction to the SOA/WHINSEC issue, this video is excellent as part of a presentation to community groups. $10.00

Thermostat, DVD with 98-page study guide. 3 hours of video clips. Responds to the question: How can we turn toward peace in a time of fear? Focuses on peacemaking 101, imagination, allegiance, security, terrorism, camouflage, U.S. tax dollar consequences and nonviolence. Available from Mennonite Central Committee, 21 S. 12 St., Akron, PA 17501. Telephone: (717) 859-1151. Web: www.mcc.org. Purchase for $25 U.S. or free loan to congregations.

War Tax Resistance, an audio tape from KFAI Radio's "Wave Project" from 2000-03-26. Linda Coffin moderated the program with Kate Coon, Judith and Dan Lundquist. Telephone: (612) 822-9714. Email: dan_lundquist@compuserve.com

The Witness, 20 minute, 16mm, b/w film. Portrays the life of Franz Jagerstatter, a young farmer in a remote Austrian village, who discerned clearly the choice between national idolatry and the will of God. Like Jeremiah of the Old Testament, he was a man who came to realize that God and the plain moral rightness of the matter were no longer on the side of his country. Because of his Christian commitment he was led to "an extraordinary act of rebellion." For his conscientious objection to Hitler's militarism he was beheaded in Berlin on August 9, 1943. Film reveals in simple moving form the confrontations this passionate anti-Nazi conscientious objector had with his family, his priest, church, and state authorities. It was produced in the 1960s by the National Council of Catholic Men for the *Catholic Hour* TV program. For a written account see Gordon Zahn's *In Solitary Witness*.

You Don't Have to Buy War, Mrs. Smith! A documentary film produced and distributed by Another Mother for Peace, 407 North Maple Drive, Beverly Hills, CA 90210.

APPENDIX K

"My People are Dying of Guns"

In Denver, where I live, who is my neighbor? No one knows who lives next door . . . That's no way to live.

The thing that was most wonderful at Wounded Knee was that we were one family. Our people came there from everywhere, all the tribes. The Lakota people were our own people, who we knew, but the other people became our people, too.

Everyone was one!

We had whites there. We had Chicanos there. We had the yellow. We had blacks there. It didn't matter who you were, what your color was, if you were a man or woman. Everyone there was a sister and brother. . . .

I am a poor, uneducated woman. I am just a poor Lakota woman.

Who am I?

But I know this: My people are dying!

My people are dying on the roads. My people are dying in the hospitals. My people are dying in the prisons. Why are they dying? Because of the crimes they have done, because of the alcohol these so-called Christians sell our men, our boys, our women. And my people are told they are guilty of this and they are punished for this. But no one says these so-called Christians are guilty for selling the alcohol. And *they* are not punished. *They* are not dying.

My people are dying of the tyranny of the white man in the Bureau of Indian Affairs. Who has taken their land? Who has left them in hunger? They are dying of hunger on my reservation.

My people are dying of guns! When the white man came here we had no guns. He brought the guns to us. He taught us to kill with guns. He teaches our young men in the army to kill with his guns. And yet the white man says: Let there be Peace on Earth. Every Christmas he says that, Let there be Peace on Earth, while he goes everywhere on earth. And he kills people.

On Sunday the white man goes to church and he prays. And on Monday he goes to work and he makes bullets with the same hands he prayed with on Sunday.

If the white man wants Peace on Earth, let him stop making his bullets. Let him stop making shotguns. Let him stop making M-1 carbines and worse guns. Then, maybe, we may have peace.

In the old days, a "good" Indian did not say anything about these things. He would be silent. He was a "good" Indian because he did not go where he wasn't wanted and he did not say anything the white man did not want to hear.

I will not be silent! I will not be silent!

My people are dying! My Lakota people are dying! My Ogalala people are dying! And I will not be silent any more!

So I tell the white man he is wrong. He is going in the wrong direction. He will be dying, too. He will be dying, too, if he does not become human.

At Wounded Knee we risked our lives for our people. For our Lakota people. For all human people. For our sisters and brothers of every people. That's a good way to live. And to die.

—Testament of Grace Black Elk, Ogalala Nation, Pine Ridge, South Dakota, of whom it was said that she did not need a gun to be a warrior. Reprinted with the permission of Vera John-Steiner whose husband died in 1987. Stan Steiner, The *Vanishing White Man* (New York: Harper & Row, 1976), pp. 191, 194-195.

APPENDIX L

Of Holy Obedience

" . . . If we were left solely to the wordy wit of legislators in Congress for our guidance, uncorrected by the seasonable experience and the effectual complaints of the people, America would not long retain her rank among the nations. For eighteen hundred years, though perchance I have no right to say it, the New Testament has been written; yet where is the legislator who has wisdom and practical talent enough to avail himself of the light which it sheds on the science of legislation?

"The authority of government, even such as I am willing to submit to, --for I will cheerfully obey those who know and can do better than I, and in many things even those who neither know nor can do so well, --is still an impure one: to be strictly just, it must have the sanction and consent of the governed. It can have no pure right over my person and property but what I concede to it. The progress from an absolute to a limited monarchy, from a limited monarchy to a democracy, is a progress toward a true respect for the individual. Is a democracy, such, as we know it, the last improvement possible in government? Is it not possible to take a step further towards recognizing and organizing the rights of man? There will never be a really free and enlightened State, until the State comes to recognize the individual as a higher and independent power, from which all its own power and authority are derived, and treats him accordingly. I please myself with imagining a State at last which can afford to be just to all men, and to treat the individual with respect as a neighbor; which even would not think it inconsistent with its own repose, if a few were to live aloof from it, not meddling with it, nor embraced by it, who fulfilled all the duties of neighbors and fellow-men. A State which bore this kind of fruit, and suffered it to drop off as fast as it ripened, would prepare the way for a still more perfect and glorious State, which also I have imagined, but not yet anywhere seen."

—Henry David Thoreau (Excerpted from *Walden and On the Duty of Civil Disobedience* with a new introduction by Charles R. Anderson. New York, NY: Collier Books, 1962, pp. 254-255) or, Staughton and Alice Lynd's *Nonviolence in America: A Documentary History*, Revised edition (Maryknoll, New York 10545: Orbis Books, 1995), 37-38.

APPENDIX M

Beyond All Price
'Our casualties were light,' the paper said
There are no scales so large that men can say
How many pounds a mother's sorrows weigh,
Or grief of a girl in love, bereft, unwed.
Man is imponderable, no thing of lead
To poise upon a balance, no thing of clay.
He is beyond all price. No gold can pay
A new-made widow mourning for her dead.

Computers cannot count how much is lost
In one whose life is snipped short in his youth.
Would he have given us new songs to sing?
What price for slaughtered music, what the cost
Of killing one who might have found new truth
To heal the body, lift the spirit's wing?

—Helen G. Jefferson, a valued and good-humored member of the Berkeley Poet's Workshop (California Writers' Club). A graduate of the Pacific School of Religion (BD 1933) she received her doctorate at U.C. of Berkeley. Her poem appeared in a magazine and was used by permission.

APPENDIX N

The Hope of the Dispossessed
"I hope that no more groans
Of wounded men and women will ever
Go to the ear of
The Great Spirit above,
And that all people may be one people."

—Chief Joseph, the dignified and eloquent leader of the peaceful Oregon tribe of Nez Perce, was instrumental in leading his people in a remarkable, thousand-mile retreat toward the Canadian border. Fifty miles from the frontier, the tribe was finally cut off by the U.S. Military and forced to surrender in October, 1877. Promises made to them were not kept, and the bulk of the 431 survivors were taken to Kansas, Oklahoma, and then to a reservation in Washington State. An indomitable voice of conscience for the West, he died in 1904, still in exile from his homeland.

APPENDIX O

John Schrag and the Burrton Incident

John Schrag, also known as "Old man Kreek-o-hannes," was a young lad of thirteen when he and his parents immigrated from Volynia, Russia, to America. They settled in the Moundridge Kansas community in 1874. The Schrag family settled four miles west and five and one-half miles south of Moundridge. John helped his father build a grain mill, later known as the Alta Mill, on the banks of the Little Arkansas River in Harvey County. John Schrag was a typical example of the Mennonite farmers in the Moundridge community who valued hard work, loved the soil, and held true to their religious faith.

Schrag was confronted with the proposition of buying Liberty bonds and being harassed by the anti-German patriots of the Burrton area. The issue came to a climax on Nov. 11, 1918, when a group of patriotic citizens from the Burrton area decided it was time for Schrag to agree to buy bonds or pay the penalty. Schrag refused to buy Liberty bonds, because to buy the bonds was to support the war, and he would not support the war. Five carloads of men arrived at the Schrag home and insisted upon talking to John. Some of Schrag's sons were home, but they refused to reveal the whereabouts of their father. The Burrton men would not take a no for an answer and proceeded to search the premises. While they were searching, they painted yellow stripes on most of Schrag's farm buildings. After some time of searching, they finally forced their way into the house where Schrag was located. Schrag did not give any resistance, feeling that to resist would only make matters worse. The intruders returned to Burrton with Schrag where he was to join them in Armistice Day festivities. A mob quickly gathered and surrounded their victim, telling him that he must buy the war bonds or face the consequences. Schrag offered to contribute $200 to the American Red Cross and the Salvation Army, but this contribution fell short of the mob's expectations. They ordered Schrag to salute the flag and lead them in a parade through downtown Burrton, but he refused to take part. A flag was then shoved into his hand, but it fell to the ground because he refused to grip it. The crowd became extremely violent and accused Schrag of having stomped on the flag. Some yellow paint was bought to the scene and poured and rubbed over his body. Some reports reveal that at this same time he was covered with warm tar and feathers. The Burrton mob justified their actions by claiming that had he not been harassed, he would not have contributed to the Red Cross or Salvation Army. Schrag was then led to the city jail where he was locked up and protected by Tom Roberts, head of the local Anti-Horse Thief Association. When Schrag was in jail, his wife tried to get in through the back window to see her husband and try to help him. Someone in the mob then produced a rope to hang Schrag, but was halted at the jail door by Tom Roberts, who was holding a shotgun. Roberts said, "If you take this man out of jail, you take him over my dead body." The mob dispersed but made plans to return later that night to hang Schrag. Schrag was placed on a chair on a raised platform while in jail so those people passing by could see him through the window in the jail's door. One member of the mob later stated that through the calmness in which Schrag conducted himself during his ordeal, "If ever a man looked like Christ, he did." That evening the Harvey County Sheriff took Schrag to Newton where he could be cleaned up and would be safe. Before Schrag was released, he was informed that he would be tried for violation of the Espionage Act.

Schrag's case was heard in the Federal Court in Wichita on Dec. 9, 1918. Five Burrton citizens presented 50 typewritten pages of evidence to prove Schrag's disloyalty to the flag. A Jewish lawyer named Schultz defended Schrag. United States Commissioner C. Sherman heard his case. The final decision, which found Schrag not guilty, was handed down on Dec. 24, 1918. The Espionage Act did not require anyone to salute the flag, and the slanderous remarks against the flag that Schrag was accused of saying were spoken in German, making it impossible to prove Schrag guilty of slandering the flag. Schrag's lawyer tried to convince him to press charges against those who prosecuted him. Schrag refused, stating that it was against the Mennonite principles of non-resistance.

The *Burrton Graphic,* the *Newton Kansan-Republican,* and the *Hutchinson News* carried articles about the Schrag incident saying that he should have been punished. The *Hutchinson News* said, "A petition was being circulated to have Schrag deported to Germany, his native land. This country is fast becoming an unhealthy place for slackers of any kind." The newspapers circulated by the Mennonites in central Kansas remained silent concerning the incident with the exception of an editorial entitled "Mob Power," which was printed in the *Herald* (Newton), edited by C.E. Krehbiel. The Mennonite community of Moundridge remained quiet concerning the Schrag incident except for some area Mennonite farmers who boycotted trading in Burrton. After this incident, the patriotic citizens did not mistreat Schrag further.

—This account is taken from a college research paper written by Don E. Kaufman while a student at Hutchinson Community College in 1968. Used by permission from *The Eden Peace Witness: A Collection of Personal Accounts* edited by Jeffery W. Koller (Wichita, KS: Jebeko Publishing, 2004), pp. 21-25.

APPENDIX P

Dear Taxpayer: The Choice Is Yours

The Earth is a free will planet in our Universe. Having freedom implies that we have choice. As persons on a spiritual path, we come to learn that we can create our own reality. We in the United States are free persons living in a free society. That is what we are told by politicians and most media; that is what we are taught in our schools; and that is what most of us believe as an article of faith. Then presumably, as United States taxpayers, we have choices. We can choose to be war taxpayers or peace taxpayers. Right? Wrong!

As a pacifist and a peace taxpayer, I am committed to the idea that my taxes voluntarily paid to the IRS be used only for life-affirming peaceful purposes. Even though the highest law of our land, the Constitution, is established in the name of the "People of the United States," it is Congress who decides how our tax money is spent. Even though the Constitution clearly states that "Congress shall make no law respecting an establishment of religion or prohibit the free exercise thereof," Congress has passed tax laws, which <u>require every taxpayer to be a war taxpayer.</u> Even though Congress has recognized the right of individuals who cannot in good conscience kill other humans by including alternative service provisions in the military draft law, there are no alternative service provisions in the tax law. Religious pacifists who take the meaning of the commandment, "Thou shall not kill" to include "thou shall not pay others to kill in thy name with thy tax money" have not been given the choice of being peace taxpayers by the United States government.

Taxpayers who wish to be peace taxpayers instead of war taxpayers sometimes feel trapped. The government requires tax payments, but makes no provision to accept taxes from peace taxpayers. If I pay the war tax, I violate my conscience. If I don't pay the tax, the IRS says I am violating the law. The IRS brands me as an "illegal protestor". How can I, as a peace taxpayer, avoid this trap? The answer for anyone who understands and believes that we each create our own reality is to define ourselves and not let others create our reality. I am a law-abiding citizen and a peace taxpayer. I want to pay my taxes to my government. It is up to the Congress, to conform the tax law to the Constitution. How the Congress does it is their problem. That is what we are paying them to do. I am one of "the people" who requires

112

Congress to represent my position of peace taxpaying. If the Congress chooses not to do this, then we have taxation without representation. As good Americans, we all know where taxation without representation can lead. By allowing others to choose for us, we are giving up power that is rightfully ours. I choose not to do this.

At this point, I can see many readers shaking their heads in fear and disbelief. How can I possibly stand up to the IRS? Won't they put me in jail if I don't pay the war tax? Won't they just take the war tax? I can't afford the price of peace taxpaying. Remember that all I have said so far is that we each create our own reality. Being spiritual does not mean being stupid. But it definitely means being honest. The first thing we need to do is to be very, very clear about what we are doing and why we are doing it. Being a peace taxpayer does not mean tax evasion. We need to assimilate the idea that as responsible citizens, we want to pay our fair share to support a government—but only a government that responds to our needs. And who needs war?

We must also understand that the IRS is simply a collection agency for the government. If we are open and honest and insist on being peace taxpayers, the IRS cannot put anyone into jail. The power of the IRS lies in the power of the purse. And as individual taxpayers, we can choose the amount of money we choose to put at risk. The specifics of how an individual can put themselves on the path toward peace taxpaying are as varied as the number of individuals. No two persons are exactly alike nor are their tax situations exactly alike. There are no limits to the ways we can choose to go. Fortunately there are organizations throughout the world concerned and working on this issue. They can provide information, inspiration, and a support system. As a founder of one such group, I promise to respond to anyone who contacts me. Remember Dear Taxpayer, the choice is yours!

—Ed Pearson, Peace Taxpayer, POB 333, Nellysford, VA 22958, or Peacetaxpayer@ earthlink.net, or Tel. (434) 361-2597.

APPENDIX Q

The Solitary Witness of Franz Jagerstatter

On August 8, 1943, the night before he was beheaded for refusing to fight for Hitler's army, Franz Jagerstatter sat in a Berlin prison cell, deep in intimate prayer with God. On a table in front of him lay a piece of paper, a promise to serve in the Nazi medical corps. All he had to do was sign his name and the Nazis would let him live.

It was a simple choice. His guards encouraged him to sign the paper. His parish priest and bishop prayed for him to sign it and save himself. His wife and three little girls begged him to give up his one-man stand against imperial violence and sign the document so that one day he could come home.

But no. He had already made his choice. He would not fight. He would not kill. He would not support Hitler's war or anybody's war in any way. And so he sat there, only hours before his execution, motionless, deep in prayer, not crying, not panicking, not overcome with fear. Franz was at peace. He was at one with the God of nonviolence.

Such was the faith of Franz Jagerstatter, executed 50 years ago on August 9, 1943, for refusing to join Hitler's army. His witness ranks him among the 20th century's most noble examples of Christian discipleship.

The scene in the cell is haunting. Who among us would have the strength not to sign the paper and be reunited with our spouse and children? Many thought (many still think) that it would have been better if Franz had compromised, at least for the sake of the children. But Franz possessed, like Jesus, a stubborn nonviolence. No compromises, no concessions, no exceptions, no deals with death—and especially for the sake of the children.

Franz took up his fear and walked into prison. "Since the death of Christ, almost every century has seen the persecution of Christians," he wrote. "There have always been heroes and martyrs who gave their lives—often in horrible ways—for Christ and their faith. If we hope to reach our goal some day, then we, too, must become heroes of the faith. For as long as we fear others more than God, we will never make the grade . . .The important thing is to fear God rather than people."

FROM HIS EARLY years, Jagerstatter had spoken against Nazi militarism. He had specifically criticized the feckless church for giving in to Nazi demands. They should have set themselves "firmly in opposition to the Nazi party," he wrote. In February 1943, he was called to active duty; and despite the urging of his friends, wife, mother, children, priest, and bishop, he refused to be complicit with the Nazis.

On March 2, 1943, he wrote to his wife, Franziska, "Today I am going to take the difficult step." His formal refusal to join the Nazi army resulted in immediate imprisonment, eventual trial, and the death penalty. In the months before his execution, the 37-year-old Jagerstatter was allowed only one visit with his wife. In his magistral letters to her, he constantly thanked her for her love and fidelity and begged forgiveness for the suffering he brought her. A few hours before he was executed, he wrote her:

> *The hour comes ever closer when I will be giving my soul back to God . . . . . I would have liked to spare you the pain and sorrow that you must bear because of me. But you know we must love God even more than family, and we must lose everything dear and worthwhile on Earth rather than commit even the slightest offense against God. . . .It is still best that I speak the truth, even if it costs me my life.*

The chaplain who visited Jagerstatter in prison the night before his execution said that his eyes shone with a joy and a confidence that he would never be able to forget. When the chaplain asked him to sign the paper, Franz smiled and gently declined. After the execution, the chaplain declared that Franz "lived as a saint and died a hero. I say with certainty that this simple man is the only saint that I have ever met in my lifetime."

Perhaps one of the most compelling images from Franz's story is the dream he had of a crowded train that everyone was trying to board. As he watched this scene, a voice told him,"This train is going to hell!" The train represented the Nazi addiction to death and Franz desperately began to convince people not to board that death train. The dream summed up his real-life experience, he realized upon awakening. "I would like to call out to everyone who is riding on this train: 'Jump out before the train reaches its destination, even if it costs you your life!'" he said.

As Dorothy Day once wrote, we can invoke Franz Jagerstatter in our life struggle to be faithful followers of the nonviolent Jesus: . . .

—John Dear, S.J. reprinted with permission from *Sojourners* magazine, www.sojo.net, 1-800-714-7474.

APPENDIX R

Truth Revealed at Nuremburg

During the evening of April 18, 1946, at the Nuremberg jail, G.M. Gilbert, as prison psychologist, continued his casual conversations with Hermann Goering. They got around to the subject of war again. Contrary to Goering's attitude, Gilbert did not think "that the common people are very thankful for leaders who bring them war and destruction."

"Why, of course, the people don't want war," Goering shrugged. "Why would some poor slob on a farm want to risk his life in a war when the best that he can get out of it is to come back to his farm in one piece. Naturally, the common people don't want war; neither in Russia nor in England nor in America, nor for that matter in Germany. That is understood. But, after all, it is the *leaders* of the country who determine the policy and it is always a simple matter to drag the people along, whether it is a democracy or a fascist dictatorship or a Parliament or a Communist dictatorship."

"There is one difference," I pointed out. "In a democracy the people have some say in the matter through their elected representatives, and in the United States only Congress can declare war."

"Oh, that is all well and good, but, voice or no voice, the people can always be brought to the bidding of the leaders. That is easy. All you have to do is tell them they are being attacked and denounce the pacifists for lack of patriotism and exposing the country to danger. It works the same way in any country."

—Excerpt from "Evening in Jail" from "12. Frank's Defense" from *Nuremberg Diary* by G.M. Gilbert. Copyright c 1947 by G.M. Gilbert. Reprinted by permission of Farrar, Straus and Giroux, LLC.

APPENDIX S

A Letter to the Internal Revenue Service

The guards at Auschwitz herded my father to the left and me to the right. I was a child. I never saw him again.

He was a good man. He was loyal, obedient, and law-abiding. He paid his taxes. He was a Jew. He paid his taxes. He died in the concentration camp. He had paid his taxes.

My father didn't know he was paying for barbed wire. For tattoo equipment. For concrete. For whips. For dogs. For cattle cars. For Zyklon B gas. For gas ovens. For his destruction. For the destruction of 6,000,000 Jews. For the destruction, ultimately, of 50,000,000 people in WW II.

In Auschwitz I was tattoo # B-7815. In the United States I am an American citizen, taxpayer # 370-32-6858. Unlike my father, I know what I am being asked to pay for. I am paying for a nuclear arms race. A nuclear arms race that is both homicidal and suicidal. It could end life for 5,000,000 people, five billion Jews. For now the whole world is Jewish and nuclear devices are the gas ovens for the planet. There is no longer a selection process such as I experienced at Auschwitz.

We are now one.

I am an American. I am loyal, obedient, and law-abiding. I am afraid of the IRS. Who knows what power they have to charge me penalties and interest? To seize my property? To imprison me? After soul-searching and God-wrestling for several years, I have concluded that I am more afraid of what my government may do to me, mine, and the world with the money if I pay it . . . if I pay it.

We have enough nuclear devices to destroy the world many times over. More nuclear bombs are not the answer. They do not create security; they have the opposite effect.

I do believe in taxes for health, education, and the welfare of the public. While I do not agree with all actions of my government, to go along with the nuclear arms race is suicidal. It threatens my life. It threatens the life of my family. It threatens the world.

I remember my father. I have learned from Auschwitz. I will not willingly contribute to the production of nuclear devices. They are more lethal than the gas Zyklon B, the gas that killed my father and countless others.

I am withholding 25% of my tax and forwarding it to a peace tax fund.

Yours for a just world at peace, (signed) Bernard Offen

—This is a slightly edited version of the letter, which Mr. Offen sent to the IRS April 14, 1986. "To all who may read this I give my permission and encouragement to reproduce or publish for sharing as widely as possible. I may be contacted c/o Sonoma County Taxes for Peace, P.O. Box 563, Santa Rosa, CA 95402.

APPENDIX T

No Reason to Fear

Ernest and I began a tax refusers' newsletter soon after our marriage in 1948. In all the time since, only a tiny proportion of Friends and other pacifists have become tax refusers, and we sometimes try to understand why. It has been, for us, more a personal imperative than a carefully reasoned political position, though we have done what we could to expound on all aspects of refusing to allow one's labor to be taxed for war and weaponry.

Most people, whether they are pacifists or not, seem to respect our "right" to refuse taxes when we have a chance to explain how we feel about it. In turn we have to accept the "right" of others to continue to pay large sums in taxes, even though the U.S. budget continues to be overwhelmingly devoted to war and the war system.

Before 1800 taxes were levied largely for specific things such as bridges, schools, highways. A levy for war was as separate as the others. Quakers, Mennonites and a few others who had strong scruples against paying for the militia or for gunpowder refused to pay and sometimes suffered distraint of goods or imprisonment for their stand. When all these items began to be lumped together into one general tax, it was no longer so simple an issue. Some, with a considerable feeling of relief, began to pay; others paid more out of frustration. And one of the most potent testimonies against war during the 1700s became lost.

Now, in 1975, probably no reasonable person believes that the billions to be spent for weapons research, deployment of armies and nuclear weapons, nuclear submarines prowling the ocean floor, planes carrying nuclear bombs, and intercontinental ballistic missiles will be in any sense a "defense" for anyone. Since such policies and practices will probably lead to a nuclear holocaust at some future time, maybe distant, maybe near, paying for these weapons comes close to being an evil act. It may be that the reason most Friends do not see it in that light is that they are conscientiously committed to liberalism—to the

119

direction the federal government began in the 1930s and from which there is now no retreat. The federal government, in order to ease suffering and to maintain control over its own populace, began to assume some social responsibility. Possibly most Friends are in the same position as those who began paying the "mixed" taxes in the 1800s. But in the past ten years the whole world has witnessed the kind of horror that a powerful military state can unleash even without resort to the ultimate weapon.

United States tax money paid for the invention and testing of hideous anti-personnel weapons. It paid for hired mercenary troops from Viet Nam, Korea, and the Philippines. Its bombers flew from safe havens to blast the fields and villages and cities of "friend" and "foe" alike. It devastated many square miles of fertile rice lands. It sent forestry experts to Viet Nam to give advice on ways to burn down the rain forests. U.S. scientists advised on the most potent chemicals to destroy foliage, and others suggested ways of seeding the clouds to cause flooding. It paid for drafted U.S. troops and got 55,000 of them killed. All this was done for reasons which no one can explain. And no one can justify. There is not a shred of legal or moral excuse for this action in Southeast Asia. In an individual such behavior would be deemed madness. Would a mad individual be permitted to continue such activities because that individual was also performing some useful service?

Another aspect of liberalism that has probably influenced Friends greatly in the past fifty years is the commitment to law. I cannot explain why most Friends think it is almost a religious principle to honor the law and the courts, while I feel it is very low on my list of loyalties. My religious instincts are insulted when I observe a judge in the robes of a priest, high above others in the courtroom, the witnesses and observers in pews and the bailiff enforcing a hushed silence. My view is that this holy-appearing scene is for the purpose of defending the property and the power of the people who have those commodities. It is the same in a socialist or a capitalist state.

It is certainly an acceptable arrangement for people to agree on certain codes or laws, agreements about property. I would not disobey laws for frivolous reasons. But I have no qualms about disobeying laws which would force me to pay for murder and other crimes related to the war system.

Civil disobedience which requires long-term adherence, such as arranging to make one's living without the withholding system, perhaps is considered impossibly difficult by many conscientious people. For many Friends, commitment to a service-type vocation seems to require "fitting in" with a professional life style. The scale has not been invented which could balance service that is beneficial to others with the negative effects of supporting warmaking and possibly silencing one's conscientious stirrings. The only contribution I can make to such considerations is my testimony that refusing to pay income taxes has proved to be a blessing in many ways. For one thing, it resulted in our "backing into" a simple life style, consuming less than we otherwise would. Friends who have valued simplicity know of its blessings—the simple life is more healthful, more joyful, more blessed in every way.

A new friend we met following seizure of Gano Peacemaker's property, our home for 25 years, wrote us after moving from Cincinnati that he supposed we were having a very sad summer at Gano this year, knowing that we would be evicted in fall. This notion was quite contrary to the way we felt. We were enjoying the time here more than ever before. The growing season seemed more productive than ever, and the surroundings more beautiful. We were working very hard, preparing leaflets, signs and press releases, corresponding, thinking of new ways to tell everyone who would listen that the IRS claims were fraudulent and politically motivated. We expected to be evicted but never had the feeling that we would "lose" in the struggle.

When, on August 28th, IRS Commissioner Alexander told Peacemaker activists at the IRS building in Washington that the Cincinnati office would reverse the sale, he said, "We're in a no-win position." We hadn't thought about it in such succinct terms, but he was right. The IRS never had a chance to win the struggle. If it allowed the sale to become final and we were evicted with our friends who would occupy the place with us, that still would not be a defeat for us. We could live elsewhere, and we would continue to refuse taxes and advocate that others do so.

One of the pleasant feelings we have about the reversal of the sale (besides knowing that we can continue to live on these two acres) is that many people have told us they got a real lift when they heard that some "little people" had prevailed in the struggle with the IRS. We had the feeling that our daily leafleting and constant public statements during the seven months' campaign had, at the least, the effect of showing that people need not *fear* this government agency. People do fear the IRS and that is an unworthy attitude. What can they take away that is of real value?

—Marion Coddington Bromley, one of the founding members of the Peacemaker movement, has had a long commitment to working for peace. This article appeared in the February 15, 1976, issue of *Friends Journal*. C 1976 Friends Publishing Corporation. Reprinted with permission. www.friendsjournal.org

APPENDIX U

War Tax Resistance

In 1945, before any of us knew that such a thing as an atom bomb existed, the United States dropped one on the unaware and innocent populace of a Japanese city. If we had known that such a weapon existed, we could have predicted, with almost total certainty, that it would be used, for where in history can we find a weapon that was built, but was not used, was produced, yet was kept on the shelf as a museum piece?

I am glad I did not participate in financing the atom bomb. My concentration, however, is on not financing the more grotesque and grisly weapons being planned today, one of them even being called the "ultimate weapon." We have indeed become a society of butchers, as Bertrand Russell said a few years ago. If this ultimate weapon should come, the ultimate danger will come right along with it, the ultimate danger for everyone on the planet. No way, then, can exist for getting rid of that danger without first getting rid of that weapon.

During World War II, I was aware that the government wanted both "you and your money." There has been a change. The government now wants your money only, for it is your money that constructs those almost self-operating weapons that can destroy everybody and everything. The government has been making it plainer and plainer that today's combat soldier is the taxpayer—the person who provides the cash to produce and deploy the push-button hardware and software for mass annihilation. The world is now spending $1.3 million every minute toward this end at the same time that it robs the already poor and destitute.

Back at the turn of the century, Leo Tolstoy showed us that individuals shouldered great responsibility for warfare. If widespread refusal of military taxes could take place, he said, something in government would have to change because government could not put that many people in prison, and, if it could, it would still be without funds for its military operations, and solutions other than military ones would have to be found. It is the same today; except that the urgency is much greater, for the "military operations" of old have now become "extermination programs."

People who contribute substantially each year to these extermination programs—and there is no way to avoid doing so when giving tax funds to the IRS—are, whether they like to think so or not, engaging in "crimes against peace," something that is forbidden by our moral code, by the Nuremberg Tribunal and by other treaties to which the United States is signatory. The excuse, "We are only obeying orders of our duly-constituted government," is, of course, empty and meaningless. The Nuremberg principles held that preparing to engage in crimes against peace is, in itself, a crime against peace, and that people cannot hide behind orders given by government when they personally commit those crimes against peace.

Those "good Germans" of the 1930s and early 1940s, who knew they were building death camps, and knew they were building those other means of human extermination, justified their acts on the grounds that they "had to obey the law." People who finance the horror weapons of today are in the same category. Disobeying a statutory law is, of course, illegal but it is not necessarily wrong. The higher laws often cannot be obeyed without disobeying some lower ones. Clearly a choice has to be made.

Holding back money from what one vitally opposes so that one can give it instead to what one vitally favors is as old as civilization itself. From history we learn that this practice existed in many parts of the world, in England, India, and the United States in the American colonies. Probably no resistance has been more effective or more honored. People in these countries, who stopped their money, cut off from government a source of revenue that government had come to depend on, and they also made clear, thereby, their open opposition to certain government laws and practices.

Our responsibility extends, of course, beyond government demands into the whole of society, and we should be ready at any time to do what we believe to be right. We are creatures of the whole earth, not just one strip of it, so, if we aspire to be citizens of something, we should aspire to become citizens of the globe. Hope for the future is dependent on many more people acting on their consciences, becoming bolder and going further than they have yet gone, for the human conscience has a power all its own.

—Ernest Bromley learned about the direct financing of war while serving as a Methodist minister in Bath, North Carolina during the 1940s. The above is an excerpt from an article written for *The Catholic Worker* (June-July, 1984).

APPENDIX V

Bring No More Vain Offerings

Last Easter I sent a check to the New England War Tax Resistance Alternative Fund to support organizations working for peace, human rights, and welfare. The amount of the check represented 18 percent of the federal income tax owed after withholding and deductions. To the IRS (and to friends, family and Congressional representatives) I sent a three-page letter explaining why I had chosen to withhold this portion of the tax as a witness for peace, as a protest of war preparations, and as an act of responsible citizenship. In deciding to redirect this small amount from the federal budget to a human needs fund, I joined some 10,000-20,000 U.S. citizens engaging in war tax resistance.

While I had become a conscientious objector during the Vietnam War and had for the past decade expressed opposition to our society's increasing militarization, I felt the need to take a further step in clearly registering my dissent. Though praising my integrity, friends and family questioned my judgment in taking on such seemingly immovable systems as the IRS and the Pentagon with a practice so obviously doomed to failure. "Doesn't this undermine our democratic system? Won't the IRS ultimately get what they're after and sock it to you with interest? Aren't there better ways of registering your dissent, like writing letters or lobbying?" they asked. Their questions merely echoed the serious doubts and fears that had surfaced since I began to consider war-tax resistance. They were the reservations which come largely from having been raised in white, middle-class America, relying on a way of life to which many of us owe our economic comforts, our college education and, to a certain extent, our health and happiness.

The bright side of this way of life Martin Luther King, Jr., celebrated in his "I Have a Dream" speech—a land of equal opportunity, freedom for all, and the right to a fair share of our resources—and is a vision I have been eager to support and defend since the days JFK spoke of a New Frontier. But there is a dark side to our way of life that, as a person of faith, I cannot support and defend, but must resist. I hope the reader will bear with me if I seem to be dwelling on this dark side and if I speak about God for a while in secular terms.

The Price We Pay for Our "Vital Interests"

It has taken me many years to begin to understand the price affluent American citizens pay in exchange for the government's defense of our alleged "vital interests." While I have long been opposed to the federal government's lopsided appropriations for military spending (roughly 53 percent of the total budget), the Reagan administration outraged me with its blatant sponsorship of military suppliers and its contempt for the poor and handicapped.

Nevertheless, it seemed easier to ignore the fact that it is from individual citizens, such as myself, that the government procures the vast amounts needed for the murderous escalation of the arms race. Though our nuclear arsenal's overkill capacity is already equivalent to the power of 200,000 Hiroshima-sized bombs, our government is currently adding MX and Cruise missiles, B-1 bombers, and Trident submarines, which clearly place us in a perilous first-strike position.

Nevertheless, it seemed easier to ignore the fact that it is from individual citizens, such as myself, that millions of dollars in military aid go to support murder, torture, and repression in such third-world countries as El Salvador, the Philippines, and Indonesia. When I learned that our government had supplied 90 percent of the weapons Indonesia used to invade the tiny former Portuguese colony of East Timor in 1975, it was easier to curse the Ford administration than to accept personal responsibility. After all, it was Rockwell International's Bronco aircraft, not mine, that was used for the incendiary bombing in 1977 and 1978 that caused the wholesale murder of civilians, destroying crops and causing mass starvation.[1] It was the Carter administration, despite its human rights rhetoric, that chose to ignore the civilian massacres and concentration camps--not me, or so I thought.

But it has not been so easy to ignore the face of Reaganomic injustice at home when the increased taxes we are asked to pay for war preparations result in a direct theft from the hungry, the homeless, the elderly, and the handicapped of our society; when the infant mortality rate among the poor is rising; when severely handicapped citizens are arbitrarily cut from disability rolls; and when a Presidential commission denies the widespread hunger and homelessness in this country. The price we pay as affluent American citizens makes us the hungriest people in the history of this earth—our greed has become so tremendous we would rather destroy ourselves than share our wealth with the poor.

Like so many others, I at first felt powerless to change these injustices. But it slowly dawned on me that my outrage came from the knowledge that these injustices were no one's if not my own responsibility, that I was a part of the sinful complicity which had permitted our government to claim such power. The words of Isaiah spoke directly to my country and to me:

> Bring no more vain offerings. . . .Your hands are full of blood. . . . It is you who have devoured the vineyard; the spoil of the poor is in your houses. What do you mean by crushing my people, by grinding the face of the poor . . . Because you have said "We have made a covenant with death, and with Sheol we have an agreement when the overwhelming scourge passes

127

through it will not come to us; for we have made lies our refuge and in falsehood we have taken shelter."[2]

During the war in Indochina, I became a conscientious objector to military conscription to register my dissent from the war machine that was destroying life there. As I began to consider tax resistance more than a decade later, I realized I was still subject to military conscription: by paying taxes without protest, I was offering my tacit consent to the death squads of undemocratic regimes that imprison and terrorize their people, to the manufacturing of more nuclear and "conventional" weapons designed to destroy life on our planet, and to the budget priorities that are "grinding the face of the poor." Simply stated, if I myself would not kill, torture, or steal, how could I pay someone else to kill, torture, and steal?

As William Stringfellow has observed:

> If it is tempting to suppose that remote proximity abolishes responsibility for killing, it must be remembered that the use of apparently anonymous automated weapons exposes the common and equal culpability for slaughter of those who pull the trigger and those who press the button with those who manufacture the means and those who pay the taxes.[3]

Praying for Peace and Paying for War

I had to face the conflict—I was praying for peace and paying for war. My "vain offerings" could not wash from my hands the blood of collective irresponsibility . . . Once again I turned to the great tradition of civil disobedience in this country; it calls upon individual citizens to hold on to the truth of their conscience and be willing to face fines and imprisonment to register their objection to unjust laws. In the words of William Durland, "unquestioning obedience to government is not part of citizenship in a democracy; it is rather the stuff out of which all dictatorships are made."[4]

In our republic, individual citizens consent to government, rendering support in the form of taxes, jury duty, voting, and civic responsibility in return for services, which are supposed to enhance the collective quality of life. I respect this "contract" and have sought, in my work with both civic and religious groups, to be an advocate of democratic values. Unfortunately, we have seen this contract widely usurped by the "shadow government."[5] This shadow government was responsible for the invasion of Grenada and the murder by air attack of two dozen Grenadians in a mental hospital.[6]

It trains and supports the security forces in El Salvador and Honduras that massacre innocent civilians; it enforces the system by which the Pentagon procures for outrageously high prices weapons systems developed by arms manufacturers; and, through our official government, it asks for our support in the form of taxes. As this national-security state was insisting upon building nuclear weapons and the sovereign right of the President to launch us into nuclear war, I began to see that we are living under a far worse tyranny than that which sparked the revolutionary cries of "No taxation without representation!"

One of the tougher questions I was asked (and continue to ask myself) is, "Aren't you irresponsibly threatening the orderly process of government with anarchy? Couldn't this kind of action set a precedent for other issues, such as tobacco subsidies or legalized abortion? Where do you draw the line?"

My refusal to pay war taxes is not done lightly or out of a philosophy of anarchy. I am not opposed to paying for such services as public education, medical care, housing assistance, transportation, and peaceful scientific research or for those nonviolent activities of our military personnel (such as the Coast Guard) devoted to lifesaving and human safety. Tax resistance is not tax evasion. I have not retained the money I withheld but redirected it to an alternative fund. In the true spirit of civil disobedience, I expect to be penalized for my refusal. I believe an important sign of the authenticity of one's dissenting convictions is one's willingness to resist openly as well as to suffer the consequences.. . .A central question can be posed: Do the services for which we pay our government ultimately enhance or devalue the quality of life?

As for disrupting the "orderly process of government," I have tried to indicate how our shadow government, in the name of national security and in a highly orderly fashion, has already abridged our human rights and political voice as citizens. As Judge Seymour Hendel told the Trident Nein during their trial for damaging a Trident submarine: "You might very well be right—that we are preparing the legal destruction of the planet."[7]

Sometimes, as in Nazi Germany or in Poland today, individual citizens are justified *and compelled* by international law to disrupt the orderly process of government. The Nuremberg Charter imposes upon citizens "the duty to violate domestic laws to prevent crimes against peace and humanity from occurring."[8] The Nuremberg Principles (unanimously adopted by the U.N. in 1950 after being introduced by the United States) forbid "crimes against peace," involving the planning and preparation of wars in violation of international treaties; they forbid "war crimes," such as the murder and ill-treatment of civilian populations and the wanton destruction of noncombatant areas; and they forbid "crimes against humanity," such as murder and torture. Insofar as the building and planning for use of nuclear weapons (whether in the name of deterrence or counterforce) threatens our civilization with total annihilation; and insofar as murder, torture, and destruction of civilian areas in third-world countries are being actively supported by U.S. military aid, individual citizens are compelled by international law and the Constitution to take steps toward prevention of these crimes.[9]

In Whom Do We Trust?

Jesus was a threat to Roman and Jewish authorities, a threat to the orderly process of secular and religious government. His

130

open defiance of inhumane laws and of moneychangers in the Temple led to his crucifixion. When asked by the Pharisees if it was lawful to pay taxes to Caesar, Jesus answered: "Render to Caesar the things that are Caesar's and to God the things that are God's" (Mk. 12:17). I believe that Jesus, in pointing to Caesar's image on the coin, meant that money is in the domain of Caesar, but that the things that are from God—namely, our life, our freedom, and our ultimate faith—are not in the domain of Caesar. Our loyalty to Caesar is subject to our loyalty to God. The claim of absolute authority made by the state and its laws cannot override the absolute authority of God's higher law.

. . .

The Great Commandment, the love of God, calls us to revere the source of all life and to refuse to pay tribute to idols. But our nation, despite the slogan on our coins, increasingly calls us to put our trust not in God but in weapons of mass destruction, gods of metal. We are called to believe in the myths that peace, freedom, and security are not God-given but ensured by a "nuclear umbrella." This is the idolatry of the state, which claims to control life and death. When we pay our taxes without protest, we are rendering more than Caesar's minted currency— we are paying tribute to Caesar's gods, sacrificing our life, our freedom, and our faith in a covenant with death.

. . . It is time to ask to what extent our loyalty to the state has over-ridden our ultimate loyalty to God. John K. Stoner writes, "In a day when the authority of the church is disobeyed everywhere with impunity, it is . . . a shock to observe the fanaticism with which Christians insist that Caesar must be given every cent he wants."[10]

Love of God is one with love of neighbor. War taxes not only raise the question, "In whom do I trust?" they raise the question: "Who is my neighbor?" As I have tried to indicate, our government's expenditures are increasingly geared toward the maintenance of an affluent minority at the expense and further oppression of the earth's poor. Our government has chosen to make war on enemies of its "strategic interests," which happen to include innocent civilians in El Salvador, Nicaragua, and Grenada, not to mention the millions of innocent civilians in the Soviet bloc who are labeled "enemy." The oneness of God leads us to the truth that humanity is one, that we are all God's children, that we are called to love even those people our government brands as enemies, as expendable. Most of us have read and heard so many shocking reports of human rights violations in countries our government supports that we often overlook widespread human rights violations here at home. While we build Tridents and send arms to El Salvador, the erosion of support for prenatal care has led to increasing infant mortality, malnutrition, and retardation among children living in poverty. As Jesus said, "As you did it to one of the least of these, you did it to me." Our covenant with death leads to the devaluing of life, not only the lives of our neighbors but our own, for we are counted among the "acceptable numbers" in the minds of defense planners.

In explaining the basis of my personal witness, I am not advocating that we all rush off and become war-tax resisters, only that we consider our loyalties and follow our conscience. I realize that many people who might envisage such an action feel constrained by occupational and family responsibilities as well as by the very same moral and legal values I have cited. I am not saying that I have found the answer and have thereby cleared myself of moral responsibility. On the contrary, I feel as though I have just begun to discover the questions that lead toward greater responsibility.

. . .

The Power and Truth of Personal Witness

In the summer of 1982, I met with a dozen long-time war-tax resisters at the Avon Institute in New Hampshire. Many of them were Quakers, but many other faiths were also represented. I was surprised to find that most of the people were in there

50's and 60's and could hardly be called political extremists. Jim and Julia Wallace, a Baptist couple from Cambridge, especially impressed me with the simple truth of their position. They were not intent upon sabotaging the democratic system but in living out their faith in Gospel nonviolence. They helped to dispel many of the misconceptions I had about being thrown in prison and harassed by the IRS. And they stressed that war-tax resistance is not a static or irreversible position. One may begin by enclosing a note with one's 1040 form, withholding a token dollar from one's payment, or refusing payment of the telephone tax, which goes toward military uses. Each person or couple has to decide what is an appropriate expression, given their convictions and financial constraints. Some, like Archbishop Raymond Hunthausen, are able to withhold roughly 50 percent of their taxes in opposition to all military spending. Others have withheld the percentage for current military spending (35 percent) or a lower percentage for nuclear weapons research and development. Because of their pacifist convictions, A.J. Muste and Dorothy Day refused to pay any taxes whatsoever. Many, especially Mennonites and Brethren, have done war tax resistance by choosing a simpler, self-sufficient lifestyle below the taxable income level. . . .

. . .

Others may differ, but the important reality for me is that I am not voluntarily giving my war taxes to the government. They are seizing them against my will. My aim is not to drain the military budget but to register my dissent. . . . In my resistance I feel more connected with my faith, my better self, as well as with a whole community and tradition of war resisters. I am refusing anonymity, claiming responsibility as a person, making peace with myself.

. . . I am convinced that, as Jim Douglass has written, "Our own sin can, through a revolutionary insight, be converted into an undiscovered energy for change."[11]

133

No, I do not believe my action will dismantle the Pentagon or the war economy. I hope it might help empower other persons—friends, family, students, political and religious leaders—to examine their own conscience and loyalties; but I am acting with the conviction of truth, not the expectation of success. Gandhi counseled us to renounce the fruits of our actions, and Jesus, who saw his nonviolent witness mocked and rejected from a cross, told us to seek first God's Kingdom. Or as the "hopelessly impractical" Thoreau wrote:

> Action from principle—the perception and the performance of right—changes things and relations—it is essentially revolutionary. . . . If one honest man in this state of Massachusetts, ceasing to hold slaves, were actually to withdraw from this co-partnership, and be locked up in the county jail therefor, it would be the abolition of slavery in America. For it matters not how small the beginning may seem to be: what is once well done is done forever.[12]

. . . My stand as a conscientious objector resulted in my working for two years in a state mental hospital. That experience, at the age of 22, changed my life, my way of looking at the world, as I came to know and identify with the rejected ones we lock up in institutions. My stand as a war-tax resister has challenged me to stand, not only at the gates of nuclear weapons factories and military bases, but with the homeless and hungry people on our streets. I have realized that the bargain I am offered as one who benefits from the wealth and resources we acquire, in large part at the cost of poverty and starvation in the third world, is an unjust bargain and must be rejected. I feel called to help redistribute those resources among the poor of the earth, beginning with myself, by adopting a simpler lifestyle, divesting myself spiritually and financially from that covenant with death that endangers our planet.

[1] See *Boston Globe* editorial, November 28, 1983, p. 14, "The Malign Neglect of East Timor."

[2] Isa. Chs. l, 3, 28.

[3] An Ethic for Christians and Other Aliens in a Strange Land (Waco, TX: Word Books, 1976), pp. 72-73.

[4] William Durland, *People Pay for Peace* (Colorado Springs, CO: Center Peace Publishers, 1982), p.12

[5] Sidney Lens, "Militarizing Democracy," *National Catholic Reporter,* November 11, 1983 (first in a three-part series) of a national-security state that has removed itself from popular control.

[6] Boston *Globe* editorial, November 3, 1983, p. 18, "Atrocity and Mistake."

[7] Quoted in Philip Berrigan, "The Gun Is Legal," *Sojourners* 12 (May 1983), p. 29.

[8] Art Laffin, "Law on Trial," *Sojourners* 12 (May 1983), p. 32 Article VI of the U.S. Constitution provides that any treaty to which the United States is a party "shall be the supreme law of the land," superseding domestic laws and the Constitution itself.

[9] Durland, *op.cit.*, pp.83-89

[10] John K. Stoner, "The Moral Equivalent of Disarmament: A Call for Church War-Tax Resistance," Sojourners 8 (February 1979), pp. 15-17.

[11] Jim Douglass, *Lightening East to West* (N.Y.: Crossroads, 1983), p.95.

[12] On the Duty of Civil Disobedience (N.Y.: Milestone Editions, N.D.), pp. 303, 305.

—Ben Tousley is a poet, teacher, singer-songwriter and hospice chaplain who lives in Wakefield, MA. A graduate of Harvard Divinity School, he is a longtime advocate of peace and human rights.

APPENDIX W

God of Nationalism or God of Truth?

Contemporary society is so complex that one encounters extreme difficulty in completely dissociating himself from it at any point. The problem of the pacifist's attempt to remove himself completely from all that is war or war making is difficult and probably impossible. The consistent pacifist should refuse war taxes, personal service, etc. A slight knowledge of economics reveals that anyone actively engaged in any productive effort is working for the benefit of the total economy, and in this case it's a war, or war-making, economy. But this does not mean that the pacifist is justified in throwing up his hands in despair and going along with war-making in all of its aspects.[1]

One meaning of the Nuremberg war trials that seems very evident is the fact that an individual is responsible for his actions and cannot throw such liability off his shoulders. Our government was one of the nations, which by this action, assented to this principle. The Nazi war criminals were not permitted to cast their responsibility on any other person or any set of circumstances.

This principle applied to us, means that we cannot throw the guilt of any injustice committed by our government or any other authority, we are held liable. We can not dismiss responsibility by saying that it was the law of the land. We cannot say that since the people in Washington passed a law or issued a decree that we are not to blame for obeying the law. We are responsible for our own actions and our own government has at Nuremberg said so!

If one intends to obey the state at all times and regardless of the nature of the demands of the state, then the state becomes God. . . .

If all persons were required by law, enacted by representative government to commit suicide upon attaining the age of 75, we should discover gross violation of the law. We should then discover that there are conditions under which all of us are willing to disobey the state. We may often act as though the state was our God, but if it came to a showdown we would deny the authority of the state. . . .

Open defiance of government seems to be more dangerous to the authority of that government than is disobedience by evasion, deceit, and chicanery. This is true because the latter type of disobedience is not motivated by principle, but by selfishness. People who violate laws by deceit may actually think that the laws are proper. They may merely wish to make exception to it for selfish purposes. The man, who openly defies law, however, is obviously out to change the law. He claims the law is bad and refuses to obey it

 . . .

The state has much power it can use . . .

The state is so constituted that it has much power over the individual. It can tax his wealth, and take his property if he refused the tax. It can make demands upon his body, and place it in prison or destroy it if the individual is unwilling to allow that to occur. But the state is not all-powerful. It cannot force a man to perform an act. God has arranged things that the individual human being is responsible for the acts he performs.

[1] Austin Regier in his statement to the court, January 10, 1949 (*The Christian Century*, February 2, 1949; also quoted in *A Little Treasury of American Prose*).

—Austin Regier, "Why Did I Refuse Registration in the Current Draft" (October, 1948 statement published in *The Courage of Conviction: The Correspondence of a Conscientious Objector.*. Edited and compiled by Susan Miller Balzer; copyright @ 2000 by Raymond Regier), pp. 207, 151-152. Used by permission.

APPENDIX X

"Of Holy Disobedience"

" . . . totalitarianism, depersonalization, conscription, war, and the conscripting, war-making power-state are inextricably linked. They constitute a whole, a 'system'. It is a disease, a creeping paralysis, which affects all nations, on both sides of the global conflict. Revolution and counter-revolution, 'peoples' democracies' and 'Western democracies,' the 'peace-loving' nations—on both sides of the war—are cast in this mold of conformity, mechanization and violence. This is the Beast which, in the language of the Apocalypse, is seeking to usurp the place of the Lamb.

"We know that 'war will stop at nothing,' and we are clear in our recognition that, as pacifists, we can have nothing to do with it. But I do not think that it is possible to distinguish between war and conscription, to say that the former is and the latter is not an instrument or mark of the Beast.

"Non-conformity, Holy Disobedience, becomes a virtue, indeed a necessary and indispensable measure of spiritual self-preservation, in a day when the impulse to conform, to acquiesce, to go along, is used as an instrument to subject men to totalitarian rule and involve them in permanent war. To create the impression of at least outward unanimity, the impression that there is no 'real' opposition, is something for which all dictators and military leaders strive. The more it seems that there is no opposition, the less worthwhile it seems to an ever-larger number of people to cherish even the thought of opposition. Surely, in such a situation, it is important not to place the pinch of incense before Caesar's image, not to make the gesture of conformity, which is required, let us say, by registering under a military conscription law. When the object is so plainly to create a situation where the individual no longer has a choice except total conformity, the concentration camp or death; when reliable people tell us seriously that experiments are being conducted with drugs that will paralyze the wills of opponents within a nation or in an enemy country, it is surely neither right nor wise to wait until the 'system' has driven us into a corner where we cannot retain a vestige of self-respect unless we say No. It does not seem wise or right to wait until this evil catches up with us, but rather to go out to meet it—to *resist*—before it has gone any further."

"   . . .

"Thus to embrace Holy Disobedience is not to substitute resistance for reconciliation. It is to practice both reconciliation and resistance. In so far as we help to build up or to smooth the way for American militarism and the regimentation which accompanies it, we certainly are not practicing reconciliation toward the millions of people in the Communist bloc countries against whom American war preparations, including conscription, are directed. Nor are we practicing reconciliation toward the hundreds of millions in Asia and Africa whom we condemn to poverty and drive into the arms of Communism by our addiction to military 'defense'. Nor are we practicing love toward our own fellow-citizens, including the multitude of youths in the armed services, if, against our deepest insight, we help to fasten the chains of conscription and war upon them."

"   . . .

"   . . .

" . . . it is of crucial importance that we should understand that for the individual to pit himself in Holy Disobedience against the war-making and conscripting State, wherever it or he be located, is not an act of despair or defeatism. Rather, I think we may say that precisely this individual refusal to 'go along' is now the beginning and the core of any realistic and practical movement against war and for a more peaceful and brotherly world. For it becomes daily clearer that political and military leaders pay virtually no attention to protests against current foreign policy and pleas for peace since they know quite well that, when it comes to a showdown, all but a handful of the millions of protesters will 'go along' with the war to which the policy leads. All but a handful will submit to conscription. Few of the protesters will so much as risk their jobs in the cause of 'peace'. The failure of the policymakers to change their course does not, save perhaps in very rare instances, mean that they are evil men who want war. They feel, as indeed they so often declare in crucial moments, that the issues are so complicated,

139

the forces arrayed against them so strong, that they 'have no choice' but to add another score of billions to the military budget, and so on and on. Why should they think there is any reality, hope or salvation in 'peace advocates' who, when the moment of decision comes, also act on the assumption that they 'have no choice' but to conform?

"Precisely on that day when the individual appears to be utterly hopeless, to 'have no choice,' when the aim of the 'system' is to convince him that he is helpless as an individual and that the only way to meet regimentation is by regimentation, there is absolutely no hope save in going back to the beginning. The human being, the child of God, must assert his humanity and his sonship again. He must exercise the choice which no longer is accorded him by society, which, 'naked, weaponless, armourless, without shield or spear, but only with naked hands and open eyes,' he must create again. He must understand that this naked human being is the one *real* thing in the face of the machines and the mechanized institutions of our age. He, by the grace of God, is the seed of all the human life there will be on earth, though he may have to die to make that harvest possible. As *Life* stated, in its unexpectedly profound and stirring editorial of August 20, 1945, its first issue after the atom bombing of Hiroshima: 'Our sole safeguard against the very real danger of a reversion to barbarism is the kind of morality which compels the individual conscience, be the group right or wrong. The individual conscience against the atomic bomb? Yes. There is no other way.'"

—A.J. Muste (Excerpted from/*The Essays of A.J. Muste*/, published in 2001 by the A. J. Muste Memorial Institute, 339 Lafayette Street, New York, NY 10012). Permission to use granted.

APPENDIX Y

Pilgrimage of a Conscience

As a student, Maurice McCrackin was impressed by the stand of the Union Seminary students who refused to register for the draft in 1940. As one opposed to war he affiliated with the Peacemaker Movement. After the war, McCrackin, pastor of a Presbyterian Church in Cincinnati, began systematic nonpayment of income taxes. In 1958 he was arrested and served a six-month prison sentence. In May 1961 the Cincinnati Presbytery suspended McCrackin indefinitely from his position as pastor. Years later he was reinstated. What follows is an excerpt of his statement to the presbytery during the trial:

> I decided that I would never again register for the draft nor would I consent to being conscripted by the government in any capacity. Nevertheless each year around March 15 without protest I sent my tax payments to the government. By giving my money I was helping the government to do what I so vigorously declared was wrong. I would never give my money to support a house of prostitution or the liquor industry, a gambling house or for the purchase and distribution of pornographic literature. Yet year after year I had unquestionably been giving my money to an evil infinitely greater than all of these put together since it is from war's aftermath that nearly all social ills stem.

Income tax paid by the individual is essential to the continuance of the war machine. Over 50% of the military budget is paid for by individuals through their income tax payments and 75% to 80% of every dollar he pays via income tax goes for war purposes.

Again I examined what the principle of personal commitment to Jesus meant to me. . . . Jesus speaks with authority and with love to every individual, "Follow me. Take up your cross. Love one another as I have loved you." What would Jesus *want* me to do in relation to war? What *must* I do if I am his disciple? This was the conclusion I reached: If I can honestly say that Jesus would support conscription, throw a hand grenade, or with a flame thrower drive men out of caves, to become living torches—if I believe he would release the bomb over Hiroshima or Nagasaki, then I not only have the right to do these things as a Christian, I am even obligated to do them. But if, as committed follower, I believe that Jesus would do none of these things, I have no choice but to refuse at whatever personal cost, to support war. This means that I will not serve in the armed forces nor will I voluntarily give my money to help make war possible.

Having had this awakening, I could no longer in good conscience continue full payment of my federal taxes. At the same time I did not want to withdraw my support from the civilian services which the government offers. For that reason I continued to pay the small percentage now allocated for civilian use. The amount which I had formerly given for war I now hoped to give to such causes as the American Friends Service Committee's program and to other works of mercy and reconciliation which help to remove the roots of war.

As time went on I realized, however, that this was not accomplishing its purpose because year after year the government ordered my bank to release money from my account to pay the tax I had held back. I then closed my checking account and by some method better known to the Internal Revenue Service than to me, it was discovered that I had money in a savings and loan company. Orders were given to this firm, under threat of prosecution, to surrender from my account the amount the government said I owed. I then realized suddenly how far government is now invading individual rights and privileges: money is given in trust to a firm to be kept in safety and the government coerces this firm's trustees into a violation of that trust. But even more evil than this invasion of rights is the violence done to the individual conscience in forcing him to

142

give financial support to a thing he feels so deeply is wrong. I agree wholeheartedly with the affirmation of Presbytery made in February of 1958, that, "A Christian citizen is obligated to God to obey the law but when in conscience he finds the requirements of law to be in direct conflict with his obedience to God, he must obey God rather than man."

Disobedience to a civil law is an act against government, but obedience to a civil law that is evil is an act against God.

At this point it came to me with complete clarity that by so much as filing tax returns I was giving to the Revenue Department assistance in the violation of my own conscience, because the very information I had been giving on my tax forms was being used in finally making the collection. So from this point on, or until there is a radical change for the better in government spending, I shall file no returns.

—Maurice McCrackin, "Pilgrimage of a Conscience" (1961 mimeographed copy, Cincinnati) as quoted in Staughton & Alice Lynd's *Nonviolence in America: A Documentary History* (New York: Bobbs-Merril Co., Inc., 1966), 307-310, or (Maryknoll, New York 10545: Orbis Books, 1995 Revised edition), 175-177. Also to be found in *Instead of Violence* edited by Arthur & Lila Weinberg (Boston: Beacon Press, 1963), 86-90.

APPENDIX Z

"Every Gun, A Theft" . . .

Every gun that is made, every warship launched, every rocket fired signifies, in the final sense, a theft from those who hunger and are not fed, those who are cold and are not clothed.

This world in arms is not spending money alone.

It is spending the sweat of its laborers, the genius of its

scientists, the hopes of its children.

The cost of one modern heavy bomber is this: a modern brick school in more than 30 cities.

It is two electric power plants, each serving a town of 60,000 population.

It is two fine, fully equipped hospitals.

It is some 50 miles of concrete highway.

We pay for a single fighter plane with a half million bushels of wheat.

We pay for a single destroyer with new homes that could have housed more than 8,000 people.

This, I repeat, is the best way of life to be found on the road the world has been taking.

This is not a way of life at all, in any true sense. Under the clouds of threatening war, it is humanity hanging from a cross of iron.

—President Dwight D. Eisenhower (April 16, 1953)

In 1956 Richard L. Simon of Simon and Schuster (publishers) wrote a letter to the president calling for a crash military program against the Soviet military threat. Eisenhower responded to Simon's hawkish notions stating that the true security problem of the day is not merely man against man or nation against nation. "It is man against war!"

"I have spent my life in the study of military strength as a deterrent to war, and in the character of military necessary to win a war. The study of the first of these questions is still profitable, but we are rapidly getting to the point that no war can be won. War implies a contest; when you get to the point that contest is no longer involved and the outlook comes close to destruction of the enemy and suicide for ourselves—an outlook that neither side can ignore—then arguments as to the exact amount of available strength as compared to somebody else's are no longer the vital issues.

"When we get to the point, as we one day will, that both sides know that in any outbreak of general hostilities, regardless of the element of surprise, destruction will be both reciprocal and complete, possibly we will have sense enough to meet at the conference table with the understanding that the era of armaments has ended and the human race must conform its actions to this truth or die."

—Printed source unknown.

APPENDIX AA

"Unintended Consequences"

In his famous study of 27 civilizations the British historian Arnold Toynbee discovered that the repeated pattern was an inability to resist military expansion. Once the appetite for battle is fostered at home, war on one frontier leads to another war just beyond to the next and the next. Supply lines get longer; the national treasury at home is gradually drained; those paying the bills begin to dissent; more and more young people are pressed into the military; anger at home turns from quiet to ferocious; the military turns from abroad to come home to stabilize the domestic situation; civil liberties are extinguished; the instinct for civilization gradually unravels. At the beginning, all those expansive and vainglorious military decisions seemed so natural. But that is how civilizations naturally decline. Once the military road is chosen it is like a dangerous narcotic and few are they who can resist.

The current temptation in Washington is to think about war like a John Wayne movie, as when a hero rode through a village of outlaws, threw a firebomb into a saloon and wiped out all the bad guys. Simple victory for the brave, the decisive, the unafraid.

Unfortunately, we just rode through Afghanistan and instead of a simplicity we left behind ministers who don't get along. One faction recently set upon and murdered the minister from another faction, on a public plane.

In the real world the unintended consequences of violence are not simple, and are often cyclical. Israel's Ariel Sharon is finding this out. Two Israelis are killed, Sharon kills 15 Palestinians. The Palestinians then kill five Israelis. Sharon kills 20 Palestinians and bulldozes a village. Violence is a dark whirlpool, it has its own logic, its downward pull toward atrocity and lawlessness, not only for Israelis, Palestinians and Afghanis, but, unfortunately now, for Americans.

The Founding Fathers were wary of militarism. They provided in the Constitution that war would be declared by the Congress, after debate, and not by the President who may enjoy too much the thrill of battle, the messianic pull. After 9/11 Congress has not made that declaration and we have not had that debate. We are "at war" according to the President, but not according to the Constitution.

Debate, were we to have one now, would surface that Iraq, Iran and North Korea are not alike and are grossly overstated to be an axis of evil. Debate would surface that many Americans do not approve bombings against civilians in Afghanistan; nor permanent detainees in Guantanamo Bay; nor suspension of the Geneva Convention. Debate would surface the grave long-term implications of military trials, suspension of due process, of the rights of habeas corpus. Debate would surface that a war to protect freedom is more convincing if the President honors the Constitution than if he ignores it.

As many as 3,000 people may have died at our hands in Afghanistan. They may have belonged to the Taliban, and they may not, it is hard to tell from an airplane. The Taliban were brutal warlords bound together by local politics. But they did not declare war against the United States. They supported Bin Laden, or tolerated his presence, but we attacked their numbers as if to be Taliban was the same as being him. Not all Palestinians are Arafat and not all Israelis are Sharon and not all Americans are Republicans and to treat any Taliban member as the moral equivalent of Bin Laden is sloppy. Unfortunately, war propaganda blurs these distinctions between combatants and civilians, between observers of criminal activity and the criminals themselves.

Another unintended consequence of militarism is that arms makers become imbedded. President Eisenhower saw it and warned us. Cost-plus contracts in America are the most egregiously non-capitalistic, risk-free, guarantee of corporate profit that campaign contributions can buy. The military industrial complex depends upon cost-plus contracts like mosquitoes sucking on children. Historically, this is not new. The British historian Arnold Toynbee in his famous study of civilizations concluded that the military in whatever country, in whatever century, always ask for more money, never less, and this is the appetite that ultimately defeats empires.

We don't have to look far for current examples. According to the Inspector General and Congressman Dennis Kucinich of Ohio, the Pentagon cannot properly account for $1.2 trillion in transactions. It has written off $22 billion worth of items as "lost." It has stored 30 billion worth of spare parts it does not need. But today the same Pentagon is asking for $45.6 billion increased spending. This is the latching on to the gut that Eisenhower believed is like a cancer. This is how Toynbee saw that civilizations spend themselves into exhaustion and eventual oblivion.

It is therefore true that the American republic has been rocked by 9/11, but not just in the way we first imagined. The inexorable logic of militarization is causing a weakening in debate, in Constitutional protections, and in a siphoning from education, from health care, from highways, and from our forests and rivers. The President calls this a militarization for freedom; but it has far more the feel of erosion of freedom. War rhetoric encourages the idea that we should be number one.

147

But civilization is not football and in civilization there is not really any number one. There is only all of us and no amount of extermination will ever overcome the ultimate requirement to get along.

—Craig S. Barnes is a multitalented person. Over time he has been an essayist, playwright, newspaper commentator, teacher, trial lawyer, politician, mediator, and international negotiator. The excerpt from "Long Range Implications of Militarism" (12-07-2004) and the talk "Unintended Consequences" (2-27-2002) are used by permission. He is the author of *Growing Up True*, a memoir (Golden, CO.: Fulcrum Publishers., 2001). His Web site: www.craig-barnes.com. A great source of encouragement and hope is to be found in his speech to the Santa Fe, New Mexico chapter of Veterans for Peace, "History Is On Our Side."

APPENDIX BB

"The War Is Winding Down"

I
The war is winding down
    (so they say).
It's not an issue anymore.
We're moving our men out
    (and our bombs in).
American lives aren't being lost
    much anymore.
"Let Asians kill Asians,"
that's our cry.
It hurts less to read about
    Asian death statistics.
"It's their war, let them fight it!"
    (Is it?)

At least we've done our part to help.
Perhaps there are a few bad side effects:
    broken families,
    destroyed homes and lands,
    lost customs and traditions,
    prostitution,
    mutilated men, women, and children,
    fear, hate, anger, distrust,
    people dehumanized by refugee camps,
    torture.
Still, we deserve some thanks for
    our help.
Never mind though;
we have work to do.
We must get ready for the
    next war.
There will be one you know.
We haven't repented yet.
II
He said,
"You speak of love,
And I see
    my home bombed,
    my family napalmed,
    my country destroyed.
    Hate!"
I said (meekly),
"But we still
    love you."
He said,
"If this is the result
    of your love,
then take it elsewhere.
It's creating a
    hell for us."

III
"Give unto Caesar
that which is Caesar's"
we often quote.
When Caesar requests,
we pay up.
But few seem very interested in what
    really belongs to Caesar.
You see, Caesar has ways of
    encouraging us.
"If I don't pay my phone tax, I may
    lose my phone."
"If I don't pay the war tax, I may
    lose my home
      or
      go to prison
(and that's no place for a Christian)."
"If I protest, I'm not
    patriotic."
So we pay up, and other people lose
    their homes,
    their possessions,
    their lives.
It's easier that way.
(Perhaps it's the Christian responsibility.)
" . . . And unto God
that which is God's"
How safe it is to skip over
    that phrase.
If we don't, there is
    conflict.
Maybe Caesar is asking for
    what really is God's.
Who gets it?
We say,

"Everything I have belongs
    to God."
If that's true, what can Caesar
    demand from us?
Can he demand
    our money?
    our complete, unquestionable dedication?
    our lives?
    the right to choose our friends and enemies?
The question then is,
Whom do we really serve?
    Caesar?
    God?
We don't have to answer;
the world already knows.
The world can see.
IV
In the beginning
    God created.
In the end
    man destroyed.
V
There is one, and only one way
    to stamp out evil and wrong
    and bring peace.
FORCE AND VIOLENCE.
It has always worked in the past
and it will continue to work
    In the future.
And a still small voice says,
"What about My way?"
VI
We pray,
"God, protect our soldiers
    in Viet Nam."

151

"God, bring peace to the
    world."
Then we write out our checks to
    IRS,
knowing that the biggest part
    of those checks
will be used to
send soldiers out to be killed
    and to
continue the war.
VII
He planted it near the road.
The soil hid its small gray form;
the root of its life stretched across the path.
It waited, expectantly,
For all elements to be present,
so it could burst into life.

A man appeared.
The root of life was triggered.
The gray form burst into life.
It threw back the covering of soil
and reached out to achieve the end
for which it had been created.
Its bloom was death;
its fragrance rotting flesh and blood;
its life was very short,
but effective and complete.
It did the work without hesitation
which its creator had designed it for.

How much better to plant flowers.
VIII
Yesterday I saw his family altar.
It was small and simple.

On it were three pictures:
two pictures were of his mother and father;
the center picture, his brother.
Only he is left alive to keep the incense burning.
His brother died in battle;
his parents were killed by a bomb.
At fifteen he is alone in the world,
a world which appears to him evil and terrifying.
I feel I must speak to him.
I must tell him,
"I did not kill your family.
This is not my war, I cannot accept it.
I will not fight in it;
I will not pay for it;
I will forever speak against it."
But can he hear?
Now in his sorrow and despair
can I expect him to listen and understand?
I am too late!
The war has turned into a monster
which consumes all.
Had I spoken sooner,
Had I faced God's challenge when I accepted His leadership,
this war could have been avoided.
Then he could have heard;
then he could have understood;
then he would still have his family.
God can forgive me,
but can my brother?
I have failed;
this small family altar is bitter proof of that.
Let this be my confession
before God and the world.
Now I accept God's challenge;
now I am ready to deal with the world

on God's terms.
Perhaps it is not too late,
but it is late.
X
A shattered primary school:
blood and splintered desks littering the floor,
mutilated bodies of small children,
terror in the eyes of the survivors,
long funeral processions,
hysterical parents burying their small boys—
all because of one small rocket.
What must be the results of a bomb
dropped from thirty thousand feet
on a school building full
of eager young children?
Does guilt become greater
as the death toll increases?
If so, those who make, and drop
the seven-ton bombs
have a great guilt to repent of.
But perhaps, rather, the guilt becomes greater
with increase in knowledge.
Some of us know
about loving one's neighbor,
God is love.
Perhaps we are the ones
who have the greatest sin.

—Max Ediger, a native of Turpin, Oklahoma, has served in Asia in a variety of MCC service assignments since May, 1971. The poem above is found in a collection of stories and poems titled *A Vietnamese Pilgrimage* (Newton, Kansas: Faith & Life Press, 1978), 81 pages. He writes: "The dusty plains of Oklahoma did not prepare me well for the savagery of war which I was to experience in Viet Nam. Shortly after my arrival I experienced the realities of bombs and rockets. As I stood among the rubble of schools and homes and helped pick up the mutilated bodies of the victims of this unwanted war, my mind churned with emotions and thoughts I had never experienced before. The only release from this agony was to write down my feelings so that I would never forget them." Permission to copy granted.

APPENDIX CC

"The Blackhorse Prayer"

On Easter Sunday 1969, Gordon Livingston, M.D. passed among the guests at a change-of-command ceremony in Vietnam for Colonel Patton and handed everyone copies of something he had written the night before. He called it "The Blackhorse Prayer":

"God, our Heavenly Father, hear our prayer. We acknowledge our shortcomings and ask thy help in being better soldiers for thee. Grant us, O Lord, those things we need to do thy work more effectively. Give us this day a gun that will fire ten thousand rounds a second, a napalm that will burn for a week. Help us to bring death and destruction wherever we go, for we do it in thy name and therefore it is meet and just. We thank thee for this war, fully mindful that, while it is not the best of all wars, it is better than no war at all. We remember that Christ said 'I come not to send peace, but a sword,' and we pledge ourselves in all our works to be like Him. Forget not the least of thy children as they hide from us in the jungles; bring them under our merciful hand that we may end their suffering. In all things, O God, assist us, for we do our noble work in the knowledge that only with thy help can we avoid the catastrophe of peace that threatens us ever. All of which we ask in the name of thy son, George Patton, Amen."

There were some high-ranking people there, including General Creighton Abrams, the commander of U.S. forces in Vietnam. There were also a lot of journalists. One of them asked Patton if that was the official unit prayer.

Dr. Gordon Livingston was arrested and an investigation was launched to see if he was a candidate for court-martial. They decided against it. It would have been inconvenient to try a West Point graduate who could testify firsthand about war crimes. So they sent him home as "an embarrassment to the command." He subsequently resigned from the army and worked with many others to end the war. They were not immediately successful. It took four years and 25,000 additional American deaths before the last U.S. soldiers finally left.

Twenty-six years later Dr. Livingston went back to Vietnam, accompanied by seventeen members of his old unit as well as his son, Michael, whom he had found there as an infant in an orphanage during the war. Nearly all traces of their having been there had been obliterated.

"As I stood on the site of that 1969 change-of-command ceremony I remembered the anger and the doubt and the fear I felt on that Easter Sunday when, with the help of a prayer, I was reborn."

—Gordon Livingston, a graduate of West Point in 1960, served as a surgeon at the height of the war in Vietnam. He received the Bronze Star for valor—and not long after, a general discharge after writing an anti-war treatise in the same spirit as Mark Twain's "War Prayer." It is documented in chapter 7, "Be bold, and mighty forces will come to your aid," of Dr. Livingston's essays in *Too Soon Old, Too Late Smart* (New York: Marlowe & Co, 2004) 38-40. Used by permission of author.

"If the war goes on"

1   If the war goes on and the children die of hunger,
and the old men weep, for the young men are no more,
and the women learn how to dance without a partner,
    who will keep the score?

2   If the war goes on and the truth is taken hostage,
And new terrors lead to the need to euphemize;
When the calls for peace are declared unpatriotic,
    Who'll expose the lies?

3   If the war goes on and the daily bread is terror,
And the voiceless poor take the road as refugees;
When a nation's pride destines millions to be homeless,
    Who will heed their pleas?

4   If the war goes on and the rich increase their fortunes,
And the arms sales soar as new weapons are displayed;
When a fertile field turns to no man's land tomorrow,
    Who'll approve such trade?

5   If the war goes on, will we close the doors to heaven;
If the war goes on, will we breach the gates of hell?
If the war goes on, will we ever be forgiven?
    If the war goes on . . .

—Text: John L. Bell and Graham Maule, 1997, revised November 2002.
Music: John L. Bell, 1997. Used with permission. 2003 Wild Goose Resource Group, GIA Publications, Chicago, IL, North American Distributor.

    The author and composer of this hymn, together with their publisher, G.I.A. Publishers, Inc., Chicago, are making this hymn available to any who wish to use it in worship. Their intention is to provide the church with a vehicle to sing its deepest fears and trepidations about the looming war, to help us in asking the questions of what will be needed to restore the world community to a state of better health, and to raise, yet once again, the as yet unanswered question, *Is war really necessary?*

The author, composer and publisher simply ask that you contribute the equivalent of a normal permission-to-reprint fee (c. $20-$25) to an organization of your choice that works for peace.

APPENDIX EE

"Beyond Vietnam: A Time to Break Silence"

... This is a calling that takes me beyond national allegiances, but even if it were not present I would yet have to live with the meaning of my commitment to the ministry of Jesus Christ. To me the relationship of this ministry to the making of peace is so obvious that I sometimes marvel at those who ask me why I am speaking against the war. Could it be that they do not know that the good news was meant for all . . . ? . . .

Somehow this madness must cease. We must stop now. I speak as a child of God and brother to the suffering poor of Vietnam. I speak for those whose land is being laid waste, whose homes are being destroyed, whose culture is being subverted. I speak for the poor of America who are paying the double price of smashed hopes at home and death and corruption in Vietnam. I speak as a citizen of the world, for the world as it stands aghast at the path we have taken. I speak as an American to the leaders of my own nation. The great initiative in this war is ours. The initiative to stop it must be ours. . . .

. . . These are the times for real choices and not false ones. We are at the moment when our lives must be placed on the line if our nation is to survive its own folly. Every man of humane convictions must decide on the protest that best suits his convictions, but we must all protest. . . .

In 1957 a sensitive American official overseas said that it seemed to him that our nation was on the wrong side of a world revolution. . . . Increasingly, by choice or by accident, this is the role our nation has taken—the role of those who make peaceful revolution impossible by refusing to give up the privileges and the pleasures that come from immense profits of overseas investment.

I am convinced that if we are to get on the right side of the world revolution, we as a nation must undergo a radical revolution of values. We must rapidly begin the shift from a "thing-oriented" society to a "person-oriented" society. When machines and computers, profit motives and property rights are considered more important than people, the giant triplets of racism, materialism, and militarism are incapable of being conquered.

A true revolution of values will soon cause us to question the fairness and justice of many of our past and present policies. . . . . A nation that continues year after year to spend more money on military defense than on programs of social uplift is approaching spiritual death. . . .

A genuine revolution of values means in the final analysis that our loyalties must become ecumenical rather than sectional. Every nation must now develop an overriding loyalty to mankind as a whole in order to preserve the best in their individual societies.

This call for a world-wide fellowship that lifts neighborly concern beyond one's tribe, race, class and nation is in reality a call for an all-embracing and unconditional love for all men. This oft misunderstood and misinterpreted concept—so readily dismissed by the Nietzsches of the world as a weak and cowardly force—has now become an absolute necessity for the survival of man. When I speak of love I am not speaking of some sentimental and weak response. I am speaking of that force which all of the great religions have seen as the supreme unifying principle of life. Love is somehow the key that unlocks the door, which leads

159

to ultimate reality. This Hindu-Moslem-Christian-Buddhist belief about ultimate reality is beautifully summed up in the first epistle of Saint John:

> Let us love one another; for love is God and everyone that loveth is born of God and knoweth God. He that loveth not knoweth not God; for God is love. If we love one another God dwelleth in us, and his love is perfected in us.

We are now faced with the fact that tomorrow is today. We are confronted with the fierce urgency of now. In this unfolding conundrum of life and history there is such a thing as being too late. Procrastination is still the thief of time. . . . We still have a choice today; nonviolent coexistence or violent co-annihilation.

We must move past indecision to action. We must find new ways to speak for peace in Vietnam and justice throughout the developing world—a world that borders on our doors. If we do not act we shall surely be dragged down the long dark and shameful corridors of time reserved for those who possess power without compassion, might without morality, and strength without insight.

Now let us begin. Now let us rededicate ourselves to the long and bitter—but beautiful—struggle for a new world. . . . The choice is ours, . . . in this crucial moment of history.

—Reprinted by arrangement with the Estate of Martin Luther King Jr., c/o Writers House as agent for the proprietor New York, NY. *Copyright 1967 Martin Luther King Jr., copyright renewed 1995 Coretta Scott King*. Also, this speech linking peace and justice is included in James Melvin Washington's *A Testament of Hope: The Essential Writings of Martin Luther King, Jr.* (San Francisco, CA: Harper and Row, Publishers, 1986), 231-244.

APPENDIX FF

"What Price Peace"

We have assumed the name of peacemakers, but we have been by and large, unwilling to pay any significant price. And because we want peace with half a heart and half a life, the war, of course continues, because the waging of war, by its nature, is total—but the waging of peace, by our own cowardice, is partial.. . . .

In every national war since the founding of the republic we have taken for granted that in wartime families will be separated for long periods, that people will be imprisoned, wounded, driven insane, killed on foreign shores.

In favor of such wars, we declare a moratorium on every normal human hope—for marriage, for community, for friendship, for moral conduct toward strangers and the innocent . . . . And we bear .. it—because bear (it) we must. . . .

But what of the price of peace? I think of the good, decent, peace-loving people I have known by the thousands, and I wonder. How many of them are so afflicted with the wasting disease of normalcy that, even as they declare for the peace, their hands reach out with an instinctive spasm in the direction of their loved ones, in the direction of their comforts, their home, their security, their income, their (future) plans—that five-year plan of studies, that ten-year plan for professional status, that twenty-five year plan of family growth and unity, that fifty-year plan of decent life and honorable natural demise.

"Of course, let us have the peace", we cry, "but at the same time let us have normalcy, let us lose nothing, let our lives stand intact, let us know neither prison nor ill repute nor disruption of ties."

And because we must encompass this and protect that, and because at all cost—at all cost—our hopes must march on schedule, and because it is unheard of . . . that good (people) should suffer injustice or families be sundered or good repute be lost—because of this we cry peace and cry peace but there is no peace.

There is no peace because there are no peacemakers. There are no makers of peace because the making of peace is at least as costly as the making of war—at least as exigent, at least as disruptive, at least as liable to bring disgrace and prison and death in its wake.

Consider, then, the words of our Savior--. . . that we comprehend lucidly, joyously, the cost of discipleship: . . .

—Daniel Berrigan, *No Bars to Manhood*, Bantam edition (Doubleday & Company, 1970) 48-49. Used with the author's permission. For multiple views of this dynamic leader see *Apostle of Peace: Essays in Honor of Daniel Berrigan* (Maryknoll, NY: Orbis Books, 1996), a tribute edited by John Dear.

APPENDIX GG

Monologue for any Friday
For Viola Liuzzo, 1960s civil rights worker killed in action

Unlike those who crucify
Or lynch or shoot and leave to die
my sin is that of standing by.

It's true I would not do the deed.
My life seems marked by love, not greed.
And yet I carry deep the seed

Of guilt because of my consent.
I know full well just what is meant
by prejudice. I might have lent

my strength in protest to the acts
of which I disapprove. The fact

that they occur and reoccur attracts

my notice, not my plan of life.
I'd stamp out all dissension and all strife,
but, God, I'd rather die than give my life.

Reprinted by permission of the author, Muriel T. Stackley, from
Oracle of the Heart (Wordsworth 2004) p. 49.

APPENDIX HH

In the Land of the Amnesiacs
Do you remember December 20, 1989?
It was the day of the apocalypse in Latin America.
It was the day the birds of prey
Came spraying fire, shrapnel,
To tear the flesh of dark-skinned bodies.
It was called "Operation Just Cause."
And just because our president wanted to show us his strength,
It came.
It went.
Just because!
No one remembers the dead in Latin America.
They died in what is yet untold reality:
We live in a land of amnesiacs
Who cannot recall death in Latin America.
And just because we live in a land where our ex-presidents
Cannot recall—
Cannot recall—
Cannot recall—
Anything about anything,
We live in a land of amnesiacs.
We do not recall

Thousands upon thousands of people
Killed with weapons made in the U.S.A.
We do not recall having sold or sent weapons to Latin America.
We do not recall December 20!
We do not remember death in Panama.
We do not recall the torn limbs of children.
We do not recall the morgues filled with dead citizens, bystanders.
We do not recall incinerated corpses without identification.
We do not recall mass burials.
And we especially do not recall the killing fields of El Playon.
We do not remember the six murdered priests.
We do not remember the Romeros.
We do not remember the Allendes.
We do not remember the women raped and tortured.
We do not remember the children we murdered
In the name of democracy.
Instead, we remember the Alamo!
In the name of democracy,
We have sponsored a holocaust in Latin America.
Countless thousands have disappeared off the face of the planet,
Yet we have never known it.
We have never known the meaning of DISAPPEAR.
And when you finish reading this poem,
You will not recall it.
You will not remember it.
It will disappear.
Just because we live in a land of amnesiacs.

—Jacob Daniel Apodaca's poem can be found in the *Kinientos Anthology*, pp. 38-39. Used with permission. The poem reveals how contradictory it is for the U.S. Government to promote democracy while exporting terror and violence.

APPENDIX II

Refusing to Pay for Killing

All forms of nonviolence are important and necessary. *The Politics of Nonviolent Action,* by Gene Sharp (Porter Sargent Publishers, 1973) lists 198 methods, including protest and persuasion, social, economic and political noncooperation and nonviolent intervention. However, Sharp observes that the vast majority of nonviolent actions involve noncooperation with the opponent. This is crucial to his premise that power over others is not something inherent to those who wield it, but is something granted by the people around them. If everyone stopped cooperating with violence today, it would disappear.

Because I agree with Sharp's definition of power, I believe that noncooperation is an especially effective form of nonviolent action. But even more compelling to me are those forms of noncooperation known as conscientious objection, primarily draft resistance and war tax resistance.

As important and effective as noncooperation with *voluntary* activities—such as buying clothes made in sweatshops—may be, I believe noncooperation with *coerced* activities carries an extra imperative. Because refusing to cooperate with the draft or taxation carries potential legal and financial penalties, such conscientious objection means not only refusing to participate in violence, but refusing to be *coerced* into participating in violence.

As a wage earner in the U.S., unless I actively refuse to cooperate, money will be withheld from my paycheck every day to pay for killing. No matter how many nonviolent campaigns I may participate in, as long as I pay my taxes I am contributing to violence. In my years as an activist I have been able to decide not to participate in various nonviolent campaigns, but I haven't been able to decide not (to) do war tax resistance. Someone once wrote to me and said he wasn't doing war tax resistance any more because it wasn't effective. To me that was like saying,

"I've decided that refusing to kill people isn't effective, so I'm going to start killing people."

Of course, I believe war tax resistance, or "revenue refusal" as Gene Sharp calls it, *is* effective. It has been around since at least the second century in Egypt. It has been used in every part of the world by people of all classes and cultures. It has proven effective in countless nonviolent struggles. Sometimes war tax resistance gets accused of being "negative," because it's about *not* doing something. People say they want to be "positive," to emphasize what they are for, not what they are against. At those times I remember something longtime war tax refuser Wally Nelson said: "What could be more positive than refusing to kill people?"

—Karen Marysdaughter, a former coordinator for the National War Tax Resistance Coordinating Committee (NWTRCC), has redirected all her federal income taxes since 1981. She and her partner, also a war taxes resister, live within a low income on a land trust in rural Maine. Used by permission.

APPENDIX JJ

What Belongs to God?

On August 6 and 9, 1945, the U.S. dropped atomic bombs on the cities of Hiroshima and Nagasaki, Japan killing an estimated one hundred thousand men, women, and children, and severely injuring many more.

The human suffering present in the stories of Hiroshima and Nagasaki is painful and sobering for all who long for a peaceful world. For Christians, the story of Nagasaki carries an added tragic irony. Nagasaki was the site of the largest Christian community in Japan. Despite years of harsh persecution by Imperial rule, thousands of Christians in Nagasaki lived and nurtured their faith in secret. Finally, in 1873 the persecution ended, and some 20,000 secret Christians emerged. These Christians built the St. Mary's Cathedral, which became a landmark in their city. At the time it was the largest Christian church in Asia.

On August 9, 1945, an all-Christian U.S. bomber crew flew over the city, and dropped an atomic bomb. Within seconds, the large Christian community in Nagasaki was vaporized. What the Imperial government could not accomplish in 200 years of harsh rule, American Christendom did in one summer morning.[1]

World War II was the first war paid for by a massive income tax, which incorporated millions of new Americans into the tax structure. Since then, American tax dollars have funded wars and military actions in a host of countries including the current "war on terror" which continues in Afghanistan, Iraq, and other countries. These wars have yielded mixed results in terms of U.S. interests, while causing incalculable human pain and suffering across the decades.

The story of Nagasaki is haunting, and leads us to troubling questions. Through the payment of taxes for war and participation in military actions, what have U.S. Christians destroyed in places like Korea, Vietnam, Cambodia, Laos, Nicaragua, El Salvador, Libya, Kuwait, Iraq, Yugoslavia, Kosovo, and Afghanistan? Have we snuffed out communities of faith who would have longed for support and fellowship? What opportunities for Christian unity and witness have we shattered? What emerging visions for reconciliation around the world have yielded to bitterness and cynicism because U.S. Christians relinquish both their youth and their dollars to fight America's wars?

If U.S. Christians were to declare ourselves free from the seduction of the sword, what new possibilities in peacemaking would await us? What opportunities to grow in our understanding of Christ's way would come to us? What suffering from war and oppression might have been avoided?

The emerging war on terror around the globe, the current war in Iraq, the dreadful cycle of violence and revenge in the

Middle East, and the ongoing pain of war in Columbia should lead us all to serious reflection. Can we join the circle around Jesus the day the Pharisees set the trap for him about whether or not to pay taxes to Caesar? Jesus told his hearers that they had a decision to make: "Give to Caesar what is Caesar's and give to God what is God's" (Lk.20:25). As noted by Willard Swartley, "Jesus' reply pointed beyond the rights of Caesar to the rights of God. God's claim and Caesar's claims must never be put on the same level."[2] As we join the circle around Jesus, let us consider the things that belong to God:

- Our work, our time, our dollars, our lives
- The call to feed "enemies" who are hungry
- The lives of all people in the Middle East caught up in a desperate struggle for life
- Our commitment to love and support our sister churches in Columbia
- Christian and Muslim communities in Iraq and Afghanistan
- U.S. soldiers at home and around the globe
- All those whose lives and minds are broken by war

As we affirm that all these things surely belong to God, how can we who follow Jesus willingly give our tax dollars for war and killing?

[1] Nagasaki story from Gary Kohls, *Every Church a Peace Church* (http://www.lewrockwell.com/orig5/kohls3.html)
[2] The *Christian and the Payment of Taxes Used for War*, paper by Willard M. Swartley, Associated Mennonite Biblical Seminary, Elkhart, IN.

—Titus Peachey, Director of Peace Education, MCC U.S. (December, 2005) Permission granted.

APPENDIX KK

"Faith and Disarmament"

As followers of Christ, we need to take up our cross in the nuclear age. I believe that one obvious meaning of the cross is unilateral disarmament. Jesus' acceptance of the cross rather than the sword raised in his defense is the Gospel's statement of unilateral disarmament. We are called to follow. Our security as people of faith lies not in demonic weapons which threaten all life on earth. Our security is in a loving, caring God. We must dismantle our weapons of terror and place reliance on God.

I am told by some that unilateral disarmament in the face of atheistic communism is insane. I find myself observing that nuclear armament by anyone is itself atheistic, and anything but sane. I am also told that the choice of unilateral disarmament is a political impossibility in this country. If so, perhaps the reason is that we have forgotten what it would be like to act out of faith. But I speak here of that choice not as a political platform—it might not win elections—but as a moral imperative for followers of Christ. A choice has been put before us; Anyone who wants to save one's own life by nuclear arms will lose it; but anyone who loses one's life by giving up those arms for Jesus' sake, and for the sake of the Gospel of love, will save it.

To ask one's country to relinquish its security in arms is to encourage risk—a more reasonable risk than constant nuclear escalation, but a risk nevertheless. I am struck by how much more terrified we Americans often are by talk of disarmament than by the march to nuclear war. We whose nuclear arms terrify millions around the globe are terrified by the thought of being without them. The thought of our nation without such power feels naked. Propaganda and a particular way of life have clothed us to death. To relinquish our hold on global destruction feels like risking everything, and it is risking everything—but in a direction opposite to the way in which we now risk everything. Nuclear arms protect privilege and exploitation. Giving them

169

up would mean our having to give up economic power over other peoples. Peace and justice go together. On the path we now follow, our economic policies toward other countries require nuclear weapons. Giving up the weapons would mean giving up more than our means of global terror. It would mean giving up the reason for such terror—our privileged place in the world.

How can such a process, of taking up the cross of nonviolence, happen in a country where our government seems paralyzed by arms corporations? In a country where many of the citizens, perhaps most of the citizens, are numbed into passivity by the very magnitude and complexity of the issue while being horrified by the prospect of nuclear holocaust? Clearly some action is demanded—some form of nonviolent resistance. . . . . .

I would like to share a vision of still another action that could be taken: simply this—a sizeable number of people in the State of Washington, 5,000, 10,000, ½ million people refusing to pay 50% of their taxes in nonviolent resistance to nuclear murder and suicide. I think that would be a definite step toward disarmament. Our paralyzed political process needs that catalyst of nonviolent action based on faith. We have to refuse to give incense—in our day, tax dollars—to our nuclear idol. On April 15 we can vote for unilateral disarmament with our lives. Form 1040 is the place where the Pentagon enters all of our lives, and asks our unthinking cooperation with the idol of nuclear destruction. I think the teaching of Jesus tells us that to render to a nuclear-armed Caesar what that Caesar deserves—tax resistance. And to begin to render to God alone that complete trust which we now give, through our tax dollars, to a demonic form of power. Some would call what I am urging "civil disobedience." I prefer to see it as obedience to God.

. . .

I fully realize that many will disagree with my position on unilateral disarmament and tax resistance. I also realize that one can argue endlessly about specific tactics, but no matter how we differ on specific tactics, one thing at least is certain. We must

170

demand over and over again that our political leaders make peace and disarmament, and not war and increased armaments, their first priority. We must demand that time and effort and money be placed first of all toward efforts to let everyone know that the United States is NOT primarily interested in being the strongest military nation on earth but in being the strongest peace advocate. We must challenge every politician who talks endlessly about building up our arms and never about efforts for peace. We must ask our people to question their government when it concentrates its efforts on shipping arms to countries which need food, when it accords the military an open checkbook while claiming that the assistance to the poor must be slashed in the name of balancing the budget, . . .

Creativity is always in short supply. This means that it must be used for the most valuable purposes. Yet it seems evident that most of our creative efforts are not going into peace but into war. . . . .

. . . I believe that only by turning our lives around in the most fundamental ways, submitting ourselves to the infinite love of God, will we be given the vision and strength to take up the cross of nonviolence.

The nuclear arms race can be stopped. Nuclear weapons can be abolished. That I believe with all my heart and faith, my sisters and brothers. The key to that nuclear-free world is the cross at the center of the Gospel, and our response to it. . . . . We are living in a time when new miracles are needed, when a history threatened by overwhelming death needs resurrection by Almighty God. God alone is our salvation, through the acceptance in each of our lives of a nonviolent cross of suffering love. Let us call on the Holy Spirit to move us all into that nonviolent action which will take us to our own cross, and to the new earth beyond.

—Excerpt from Archbishop Raymond Hunthausen's now-famous speech given on June 12, 1981, at the Pacific N.W. Synod

Convention of the Lutheran Church. The full text is printed in chapter 4 of William Durland's manual, *People Pay for Peace: A Military Tax Refusal Guide* (Colorado Springs, CO 80901: Center Peace Publishers, 1982), 50-52. Used with permission.

APPENDIX LL

"They'll Buy No Bombs"
(Tale of Maurice McCrackin)

'Twas in September of fifty-eight

1) The tax men came up to my gate.
   They said, "McCrackin, we want you;
   Your income tax is overdue."
   I'd spent my time, as preachers should—
   To try to save my neighborhood.
   Now I'm in jail, six months to do.
   I told Internal Revenue.

   Chorus

   Tear up that income tax return;
   They'll buy no bombs with what I earn.
   If they want money, they can go down
   To the banks of the Ohio.

2) I'd not support a prostitute,
   Nor buy some thug a gun to shoot
   Why should I buy a war machine
   To kill a child I'd never seen?
   Don't bail me out, don't pay my fine;
   There's no one's blood I want to spill
   And I'll not pay a war-lord's bill.

   Chorus

3) The ones who plan for blood and strife
   Demand my money or my life;

172

My faith in God is not for sale
That's why I'm here, locked up in jail.
But through these bars, I see blue sky,
I know that someday you and I
Will both be free from hate and war—
And that's the day I'm working for.
                    Chorus

—Lyrics rewritten by Ernie Marrs (1932-1988); tune adapted from "Banks of the Ohio." Marrs arranged his version based on a song that was already in circulation, although it was frequently credited to him. Actually, two West Coast musicians, Ed Rush and George Cromarty, who were members of the Goldcast Singers, wrote it. Ed Rush traced the song back to an African-American camp-meeting song with lyrics "I don't care if it rains or freezes, leaning on the arms of my Jesus," which was the theme song of a religious program broadcast from Baton Rouge in the 1940s (Broadside # 41) Text and quotes extracted from the notes by Jeff Place accompanying The Best of Broadside. Copyright 2004 Smithsonian Institution.

APPENDIX MM

Nellie Lehn – Another Life That Made a Difference

I have often wondered why Cornelia Lehn's life turned out to be so special, so unique. True, she was born in the Ukraine in 1920 during a time of civil unrest. A revolution was in process. Important decisions had to be made by her parents and her community of faith. In her sister Sara's biography (*Ever Into New Horizons*), one learns that the prospect of dying was near at hand. She reports that "One bullet came right through the window of our back room and made a hole in the opposite wall – just above the cradle where our Baby Frieda was sleeping. . . ."

(p. 13). This didn't happen to Nellie but I suspect the story was told and retold often.

After relocating to a Saskatchewan farm with her parents, Cornelia was the only Mennonite child in that school. Because she appeared to dress and speak differently from others, her classmates had taunted her. Bewildered by their non-acceptance she inquired of her father, "What is a Mennonite?" His answer, thoughtfully and lovingly given, made a lasting impression. He said: "To be a Mennonite means to study the Bible seriously and then to obey the Word regardless of the consequences."

During the 1940s when she was a student in a British Columbia high school her Mennonite faith was severely tested. She agonized over the inconsistency of those who encouraged their sons not to enlist in the military but who supported the war by purchasing bonds. Although she desperately wanted to be accepted by her peers, Nellie decided not to donate the ten cents required each week in the school war-bond drive.[1]

During the Vietnam War years Nellie became increasingly troubled about supporting death and destruction in Southeast Asia through her payment of taxes. A poster showing a grim scene of suffering with the caption "Your Tax Dollars at Work" affected her deeply. She struggled to reconcile the biblical injunction to pay taxes and the clear commandment to love one's enemies. In 1977 she told her story to delegates and visitors at a conference. This led to more discussion. Through her open and unpretentious manner she won the respect of others. As a 'professional' she refused to abide by the rule that one must remain silent. In this way her witness became a bold and winsome expression of how Christians connect with and triumph over the harsh realities of life.

No longer able to be a part of something so diabolical as war, Nellie did the honorable thing. She spoke out against the folly of military power and refused to pay the war taxes. Instead she devoted her energies and resources to peacemaking. She made it her practice to give large portions of her income to church work. Moreover, she collected fifty-nine stories from the past 20 centuries which show us how we, too, can make peace. For Nellie's faithful witness to the "Good News" we can all be grateful. One of her six books declares, *Peace Be With You!*

Fortunately, her witness for peace lives on, inviting us to say to government, "We will not give you our sons and daughters, and we will not give you our money to kill others. Allow us to serve our country in the way of peace."

[1] Edna Krueger Dyck, "She Studies and Obeys," *Builder 31* (Jan. '81), 12-13.

—Donald D. Kaufman lives in Newton, Kansas. His tribute was written to honor this winsome lady born in the Ukraine.

APPENDIX NN

"Standing in a draft"

[According to the Selective Service System, if and when the Congress and the President reinstate a military draft, the Selective Service System would conduct a National Draft Lottery to determine the order in which young men would be drafted. The lottery would establish the priority of call based on the birth dates of registrants. In 1988, when this article was written, those turning 26-34 were still liable for induction and the author had just turned 35 and was no longer "standing in a draft."]

Growing up in a Mennonite community in southeastern South Dakota in the 1960s was a mix of security and confusion. I remember my father phoning the one-room schoolhouse where I was a fifth grader and telling me that President Kennedy had been shot. His successor, Lyndon Johnson, was the person most responsible for the Vietnam War.

I sometimes joke about having grown up with "kerosene TVs," but there is no question that TV coverage of the Vietnam War made it difficult to ignore. And turning 18 was a difficult coming of age.

Mennonites in my part of South Dakota had worked their way through two world wars and the "Korean conflict." A number of my classmates and I had been born during our fathers' 1-W work (alternative service) in the early 1950s.

Still, there was and is in this community a strong vein of nationalism and patriotism. With the shedding of the German language, debates about anti-communism were far more frequent than debates about Anabaptism. This embrace of God and country created tension for those of us approaching draft age.

The controversy centered on the extent of cooperation with the Selective Service System. John D. Unruh, in *A Century of Mennonites in Dakota*, says that in World War I 89 percent of the South Dakota Mennonite draftees were either conscientious objectors or non-combatants, while in World War II the figures dropped to less than 50 percent. During the Vietnam War no apparent disapproval was given to joining the armed forces when drafted. But prior to being drafted and subjecting themselves to the nation's biggest lottery, all males had to register with the SSS upon their 18th birthdays.

The options were simple. You could register as a conscientious objector, await the lottery and hope for a high draft number. You could refuse to register and head for Canada. Or you could refuse to register and protest.

My concerns with registering are the same today. Should one cooperate with a system set up primarily to train people to kill (euphemistically expressed as "defending your country")? Conscription (which is the only reason for registration in the first place) is the antithesis of voluntary service. The community generally opposed non-registration. The fact that CO status was conferred almost automatically upon Mennonites who applied made questioning registration a non-issue for most. (Although

Manitoba is a reasonable distance from South Dakota, I know of no one from my community who moved to Canada.)

I thought long and hard about the protest option. If war is wrong, what were Mennonites doing cooperating with a system that was methodically bombing poor Southeast Asian countries back to the Stone Age?

The military trains young men as a unit, then turns them loose in situations where survival is dependent on killing to keep one's buddies and oneself from being killed. No comparable support group existed in the community for those wishing to challenge this system.

Lack of support, or lack of nerve, found me in Salem, S.D., a concerned but confused 18-year-old, warily registering my whereabouts with a government that would have cheerfully and at great expense taught me 50 ways to kill.

But, as the poet says, one need not go quietly into that dark night. I had registered as a CO. But we lived just across the border in McCook County, where Mennonites were few. This draft board seemed taken back at my supplementing my file with anti-war articles and such. They denied my request for CO status.

I appealed this decision. Virgil Gerig, the minister at the Mennonite church I attended, and Don Klassen, a deacon there, assisted me at the appeal hearing. I was prepared for anti-pacifist questions but was floored to be closely questioned as to whether I was behind what to them was an anti-war conspiracy in the county. It seems that a lot of young men in the county had also sent anti-war material to the draft board. This was the first I knew how unpopular the Vietnam War was. It reinforced my feeling that by remaining silent the Mennonite community had lost an opportunity to witness to the larger South Dakota population.

With my CO status finally granted, I sat around a Freeman Junior College dorm room with other classmates the day of the lottery. All the dates in a year were dumped into a fishbowl, and

177

birthdays were pulled to match numbers 1-366. Odds were that anything above 200 would probably be safe.

The draft lottery was the only lottery I've ever won. I got number 45, meaning that conscription was not far away. I was ordered to Sioux Falls for an induction exam. Some tried to flunk either the physical or intelligence portion of the test, but I took particular effort to make a high score to show that this was one smart cookie they weren't going to see in boot camp.

After the exam a colonel came in with a photographer wanting publicity shots, and in an offhand fashion asked if anyone objected to being photographed. While most of the group were pumping up their chests, I raised my hand and asked to be excused. From the look on the colonel's face, I could just as well have been marched off to a firing squad.

Roughly six months before I was due to be drafted, President Nixon installed the novel concept of the volunteer army. My growing anxiety about further cooperation with the SSS vanished in one swift stroke.

Now in Seattle, the shadow of the SSS has been officially lifted. But its spirit is not dead. The issue of non-cooperation is still alive, but the entity is now the Internal Revenue Service and its insistence that while the SSS no longer needs my body to kill for it, by God (referencing the God they Trust) the government needs my money to do the same thing. To date, the answer is different than when I was 18. Here in Seattle there is support, and the answer for my wife and me has been "no." We will not cooperate. We will resist. We will lobby for a U.S. Peace Tax Fund Bill and will encourage others to do likewise. (The counterpart north of the 49th parallel is Conscience Canada.) Without encouragement and support and witness we are not a community.

—David E. Ortman, 7043 22nd St. NW, Seattle, WA 98117, attends the Seattle Mennonite Church. His revised article is used with permission. Also he authored a poem on the theme of "working for the war machine" which appeared in the *Freeman Courier* (Sept. 26, 1990, Vol. 90:25, Letter-to-the-Editor, page 4). It was written in response to news that the Mennonite community of Freeman had a local company that was bidding on Pentagon contracts!

APPENDIX OO

The Siamese Twins of Militarism

Two of the most obvious characteristics of Canada and the United States today are (first) our affluence and (second) the extensive and increasing militarism of our societies. The US is foremost in the world in terms of military spending compared to the (per capita) Gross National Product, while Canada ranks 22nd of 140 nations by the same measure (Ruth Leger Sivard, *World Military and Social Expenditures,* 1979). The US has with Selective Service registration taken the first step toward resumption of conscription.

Conscription for military service occurs in 1981 in the context of a growing understanding that militarism in both US and Canadian societies is supported far more directly by the ongoing conscription of income taxes for war purposes than by the induction of a few hundred thousand young people out of several millions eligible. The military significance of training an additional US Army division at Fort Riley, Kansas, for example, pales in comparison with the potential devastation of the Titan II missiles in place near Mennonite farmland around Wichita, Kansas. Those missiles were bought and paid for by the US taxpayers of 20 years ago. Today's taxpayers have bought such awesomely more destructive nuclear weaponry that even Kansas's hawkish Senator Robert Dole has questioned whether the 1,054 Titans aren't "superfluous." The same is true for the BOMARC air defense missiles formerly scattered across Canada.

The central problem in 1981 is not the draft; it is militarism. Our understanding of this reality is crucial to a review of our 20th-century Mennonite history in North America. Failure to recognize the root problem of militarism may bring us dangerously close to believing that the previous patterns of conscientious objection expressed in alternative service will automatically suffice in the present situation.

The danger we face as Christians is we have allowed ourselves to believe that the alternative service we have done as conscientious objectors under the compulsion of conscription is Christian service. It is not. Service by Christians is service and not servitude only if it is freely given in response to the grace of God in Jesus Christ.

This statement is not meant to deny that acts of Christian service to individuals can, and did, *frequently* occur in every situation, even that of alternative service compelled by conscription. Ephesians 6:5-9 calls us to precisely such service, even if the situation is that of slavery to a human master: "Slaves, be obedient to those who are your earthly masters, with fear and trembling, in singleness of heart, as to Christ; not in the way of eye-service, as men-pleasers, but as servants of Christ, doing the will of God from the heart, rendering service with a good will as to the Lord and not to men, knowing that whatever good any one does, he will receive the same again from the Lord, whether he is a slave or free. Masters, do the same to them, and forbear threatening, knowing that he who is both their master and yours is in heaven, and that there is no partiality with him."

Christians are always called to subject themselves in service to one another (Ephesians 5:21), and even to persons who are not Christians, "for the sake of conscience" (Romans 13:1-7). "Conscience" here means "co-knowledge." "Aware of God the Father of all, of Christ the reconciler of all, and of the Spirit's irresistible power, the Christians are free to serve, to bear, and to stand." Note that our willing subjection, or respect, is to the *person*, not the office or the law behind the office. Romans 13:7

says "honor to *whom* (not which) honor is due." (I am indebted for my comments on Ephesians [and Romans] to Markus Barth, *The Broken Wall: A Study of the Epistle to the Ephesians,* Judson Press, 1959, pages 169ff.).

A misplaced honor or respect to the institution of conscription or laws requiring universal military training fails to let the rulers and authorities know that war is not the will of God. . . .

If, accepting alternative service restrictions under governmental regulations, we do not have the "boldness" to let the ruling authorities know that peace is the will and plan of God, then we have come dangerously close to following "the way of eye-service," and becoming "men-pleasers" (Ephesians 6:6).

Can it be that this misplaced respecting of institutions and laws rather than persons has come about because we have put the burden of Christian witness on 18-to-20-year-olds, who are perhaps least prepared through experience to detect the difference?

Can it be that because of the risks to ourselves and our security, we who are older have failed to acknowledge that conscientious objection to military participation and conscientious objection to war taxation are Siamese twins? Just because we may have become too old to be liable to the draft does not mean our contribution to warfare is ended. We continue to serve the military through conscription of our taxes.

. . .

. . .

(The challenge which we face requires) a new option, a new model for Christian service in the midst of the demands of militaristic societies. Our proposal must be directed first to the church, and secondarily to the US and Canadian governments. It must strike a new stance in the political arena where the demands of the state and the call of God overlap and frequently conflict.

. . . By acknowledging that we as Mennonites ought to face together the Siamese twins of military conscription and war taxation, which spring from the parent, militarism, we can unify the generational differences in our congregations.

. . .

So the Peace Tax Fund bills speak effectively to the war taxation twin. They speak to the military conscription twin as well by defining as "eligible" taxpayers those classified as conscientious objectors.

If it is true, as General Lewis Hershey and numerous US Selective Service documents have claimed, that the CO provisions of 1940-75 were a good accommodation strategy for the US government (by avoiding a direct confrontation with the peace churches as in World War I), then one wonders why the US legislators and Canadian MPs have not rushed to establish Peace Tax Funds and thereby avoid confrontations with the war tax objectors.

Certainly one part of the answer is that our governments know that the peace churches are not unified on this issue, and they can continue to deal with individual objectors quietly and piecemeal in Internal Revenue Service and Revenue Canada offices.

But perhaps the stronger reason is that taxation is more important for a high-technology military establishment than manpower. Peace Tax Fund bills allow the taxpayers some choice in directing the spending of their taxes. This could, as the minds of many legislators conceive, "open the floodgates" to a deluge of what they look upon as "special interest legislation." Most of such tax legislation, or "loopholes," is written to financially benefit individuals, groups, or corporations.

. . .

. . .

For this reason, a "Sabbatical Service Act" may have considerable appeal in the US Congress or Canadian Parliament where the Peace Tax Fund bills alone have not. How can one consider that a people who are willing to accept seven years of service spread throughout their working lives, and thus accept substantial limits on their income growth, are seeking "special interest legislation"? Are such a peculiar people unpatriotic, who are willing to reduce the benefits they receive from North American economic systems in return for recognition of their conscientious objection to military service and military-purposes taxation?

—Robert Hull came to peacemaking out of a military tradition. He served as secretary of peace and justice for the Commission on Home Ministries of the General Conference Mennonite Church for 15 years (Aug. 1, 1979—Nov. 15, 1994). During this time he also edited the *God and Caesar* Newsletter. The excerpt above is taken from his two-part article on "Sabbatical Service" (*The Mennonite* 96:05, Feb. 3, 1981), pp. 68-70. It is used with the author's permission.

APPENDIX PP

"War Tax Resistance and Me

In December of 1990, I became a war tax resister. Shortly before the Persian Gulf War (#1), I attended a peace rally on the Boston Common. Despite the impassioned speeches given by Howard Zinn, Daniel Ellsberg, and others that day, I had a sinking feeling that standing out in the cold for a few hours, chanting slogans, and marching through the streets of downtown Boston was not going to stop the war from happening. After all, why should President Bush care that my toes were frozen and my voice was growing hoarse. But sometime during that afternoon, a young woman handed me a half sheet of paper. On one side was a quote from Alexander Haig, Secretary of State, during the Reagan administration—"Let them march all they want, as long as they pay their taxes." That quote hit me; it really hit me. On the other side of the paper was an announcement for a meeting to discuss how one could refuse to pay for the upcoming war and redirect the money to organizations that work for peace. The idea seemed so simple, so elegant, a child could understand it: don't pay people to do bad things; pay them to do good things. I had been groping for a way to step up my level of resistance to US military violence, and this seemed to be exactly what I was looking for. I was determined not to be a mere bystander with respect to the impending war with Iraq, and WTR seemed to be a way to say "No!" in a manner the Al Haigs of the world would understand.

There were other, deeper, more personal reasons why WTR seemed "right"—right for me. Because of my family history, I feel that I have a special debt to pay to people of conscience, people who choose not to cooperate with state-sponsored murder. My parents, grandparents, and other relatives were forced to flee Nazi-occupied Europe during WWII. Being Jews, their lives were in danger, and on numerous occasions their lives were saved by people who protected and hid them, who warned them of raids and roundups by the Gestapo and their collaborators, who provided them with false identity papers, and who eventually helped them enter Switzerland illegally and thus to relative safety. The people who did these things for my family took great risks. Some of their names I know from stories my grandparents told me; others remain anonymous. Their acts of compassion were strictly illegal: if they had been caught sheltering Jews, they could have been sent to the concentration camps along with the captured Jews, or even killed then and there. I cannot thank these people—most of them are probably dead by now, or very old. But to honor them, I can strive to be a little bit like them. I, too, can choose not to cooperate with murder, even if such non-cooperation is deemed illegal by the state—which it is in the case of WTR. Today, I am confronted by the same choice that confronted the gentile bystanders of Europe: Do I remain silent? Do I look the other way?

Do I say, "It's not my problem"? Do I obediently pay war taxes so that others can kill in my name? Or do I say, "No!" and break the law in the hope of saving someone's life? I owe it to the people who saved my family to choose this last option.

To become a war tax resister is, in some sense, to step into another world. "It will change your life," a fellow resister said to me early on, "but it will be a blessing." He was right. WTR has forced me to think about what is meant by the word "security." In a society as heavily monetarized as ours, security often translates as "financial security." Examining security has led me to ask the questions, What do I really need? What is truly my share? Are there ways of obtaining the things I really need without recourse to money?

What if the absolute "worst" happens and the IRS seizes my income and my savings? —not likely, because they are supposed to leave you with something to live on. But supposing it did happen. Would I be destitute? Homeless? Hungry? I think not. Friends and family would not let me live on the street, just as I would not let a friend or family member of mine become destitute in this way. People would help me out until I could get my life back together again. One would discover under such circumstances that security is not predicated by how much money one has in the bank or whether one has invested in various "insurance companies." Rather, real security, to the extent that it exists at all, has more to do with mutual aid, with friends, family, community, helping and supporting one another.

Furthermore, it must be acknowledged that, whatever the bad consequences are that could conceivably happen to me as a result of WTR, they are nowhere near as bad as what happens to people who are on the receiving end of U.S. (or U.S.-sponsored) militarism. The risks of not paying war taxes are overshadowed by the risks of paying them. I've decided that I would rather suffer than be complicit in the suffering of others—or worse, be an accessory to murder. Still, even as a war tax resister, my hands are not clean. . .

185

Indeed, WTR has made me think about the violence inherent in our economy, the myriad connections between money, greed, and violence. The more aware I become of the violence connected with economic activity—virtually all economic activity—the more I strive to live outside the mainstream economy—a difficult struggle, to say the least. This awareness, I feel, is the greatest gift, the greatest blessing, of WTR. If I have the courage to act on it, it brings me closer to the type of nonviolence that Gandhi lived and talked about: what my friends the Nelsons have termed "the nonviolence of daily living." WTR has helped me to live a more examined life, to seek out the root causes of war and violence and not just react to its ugly, outward manifestations. This has led me, more recently, to conclude that WTR, though necessary, is not enough. War taxes indeed constitute one of the principal resources of war, but they are not the source of war.

The true source of war in our time, as I see it, is none other than the American Way of Life—a way of life founded on and maintained by taking through force things that do not rightly belong to us, whether that be Native American land, or the labor of people of color, or 50% of the world's resources (used up by less than 5% of the world's population), or access to the markets, and thus the wealth, of other nations worldwide. Many in the peace movement are familiar with the slogan, "no justice, no peace," but if they really thought through the meaning of those words, they would have to confront the reality that we in this country cannot go on living the way we do. A mode of living dependent on exploitation and injustice cannot add up to peace, no matter how many streets are "taken to," slogans chanted, songs sung, sit-ins sat, or even taxes redirected.

My understanding of nonviolence also forces me to admit that I am relatively powerless when it comes to changing the behavior of other people. My influence on others, while not zero, is quite limited. However, I have considerable latitude when it comes to changing my own behavior, and as far as this is concerned, I will have my hands full for a *looong* while yet. But I credit WTR, and individual resisters I've met, for setting me on this long, fascinating, difficult, risky, arduous, rewarding, surprising, and ultimately liberating journey.

—Aaron Falbel lives in Western MA and is an organic gardener and a part-time librarian. His profile essay appeared first in *More than a paycheck* (April 2003), 5-7. Used by permission.

War and Complicity

There used to be a time when the phrases "U.S. imperialism" and "the American empire" were uttered only by people on the far left of the political spectrum. Nowadays, someone like Michael Ignatieff of Harvard's Kennedy School of Government can write a cover story for *The New York Times Magazine* entitled "The American Empire (Get Used to It)," or Jay Tolson in *U.S. News & World Report*, "The American Empire: Is the U. S. Trying to Shape the World? Should it?" Imperialism is now the duty and the burden of the last remaining superpower on the planet. How times have changed!

It's all out in the open now. There is no longer any attempt to conceal the fact that life in the U.S. depends upon the exploitation of people around the world. Exploitation, after all, is the business of imperialism—it's what empires do. We exploit others for their labor, their markets, and, especially, their resources. In particular, our economy has developed a voracious appetite for fossil fuels, especially oil and natural gas.

However, world oil production is now at its peak. From now on, production will decline. (Natural gas production in North America has already peaked.) As our empire literally runs out of gas, it will lash out even more violently to secure control of the last remaining reserves of fossil fuels on the planet. It must do this if it is to sustain our economic dominance and high-consumption way of life. That's what the "resource wars" of the past few decades are all about. That's why we have so many military bases around the world.

<u>You and I are both part of the empire.</u> We are complicit in these wars insofar as we benefit from them, insofar as our level of consumption is their raison d'entre. It's too easy to blame everything on George W. Bush and a bunch of other bad guys in Washington. Besides, the power exercised by the Bush administration and its corporate backers comes from <u>us</u>. We buy their products and services; we pay their taxes. The blood is thus on our hands as well: it flows into our gas tanks and splatters virtually every purchase we make.

`If the violence of our empire shames and distresses us, we can abate it only by addressing its root cause: our own level of consumption. *We can decide to consume less . . .and consume wisely!* We can scrutinize everything we eat, everything we wear, every consumer good we purchase that masquerades as a necessity, and ask the following questions: Who produced this? Under what circumstances? With what impact on nature? How far did it travel to get to me? Answering such questions may not be easy, but if we are serious about stemming the violence of our empire (and not just complaining about it), then this is homework we must not shirk. We can also ask ourselves questions that do not require any research: Do I really need this? Do I really need to take the car? Do I really need to use this electrical appliance or gadget? You and I can deflate the empire through the practice of self-limitation. This may prove to be good for the economy, but it's clear that our overgrown, bloated economy is bad for <u>everyone</u>. We can disarm our violent empire only by disarming its predatory economy.

Economic shrinkage may cause unemployment and dislocation, especially for the most vulnerable members of society, but <u>it will happen anyway</u> (and with a vengeance!) as the age of fossil fuels comes to an end.

The sooner we make the transition from a massive, exploitative global economy to many small, regional, limited, local economies, the less suffering there will be. The longer we wait, the more pain, suffering, war, and violence we can expect.

We can also refuse to provide financial support to the military machine: i.e., war tax refusal. If we do not support the wars of our empire with our minds and our hearts, then why support them with our wallets? You and I can decide not to sponsor the "defense" of a morally indefensible way of life—a way of life that is ultimately suicidal.

However, let our first priority be to take steps to disengage from this way of life ourselves. Only then can we reduce our complicity in war. Only then can we begin to distance ourselves, morally and economically, from membership in the empire.

—Aaron Falbel is a resident of Western MA and works in the capacity of an organic gardener and a part-time librarian. The text was originally used as a Tax Day leaflet in Greenfield, MA., and subsequently published in a newsletter put out by the Catholic Peace Fellowship in Philadelphia, PA.

APPENDIX QQ

False 'honor'
The most heavily weaponed submarine ever built cost $3.2 billion and is named the *U.S.S. Jimmy Carter.* At the Feb. 19, 2005, commissioning ceremony, Carter said, "The most deeply appreciated and emotional honor I've ever had is to have this great ship bear my name."

Although Carter is a professed follower of Jesus ("Former President's View of War, Faith, Politics," Nov. 14), a Baptist Sunday School teacher, a longtime volunteer for Habitat for Humanity, an acclaimed human rights advocate and liberal

189

Democrat, he demonstrates to the world that there's not a dime's worth of difference between Democratic and Republican politicians when it comes to murdering multitudes of people worldwide for the U.S. Empire.

On March 3, I wrote Carter a letter, to which I have received no reply. In part it read: "I am 59 years old. My mother and I voted for you in 1976. If you claim to follow Jesus, how can you celebrate having a submarine named after you, a submarine prepared to mass-murder multitudes of moms, dads and children? I would be ashamed . . .to have any weapon named after me. I have paid no federal income tax for 26 years. I refuse to pay for war. I have no right to pay tax to do to other people what I do not want them to do to me . . .

"I refused to be a soldier in 1969 during the Vietnam War. For me, as a conscientious objector, to pay federal income tax to train other Americans, largely the poor and people of color, to become professional hired killers to murder on command with no conscience, would be more evil than being a soldier myself.

"My life is an all-out public boycott of the U.S. Empire everyday as long as I live."

No job, no salary, no relationship, no degree, no house, no car, no art, no furniture, no trip, no gadgets, are worth paying federal income tax to rob, terrorize, blind, cripple, paralyze, make homeless and murder our sisters and brothers worldwide.

The main purpose of the U.S. war machine is to make sure that most Americans, especially the greediest, keep on stealing and hogging the wealth of the world.

The best way to boycott the U.S. war machine, with no fines and no threats from the IRS, is to live simply—under the taxable level.

The taxable level this year (2004) for a single, sighted, under 65-year-old person is $7,950. I lived well last year on $3,390.

. . . If a father gives his son a switchblade, how can the father be shocked if his son eventually stabs someone? Many

190

U.S. peace activists for decades have paid thousands of dollars to the U.S. war machine. So, how can they be shocked when the U.S. Empire uses the weapons purchased by the peace activists to mass-murder worldwide? We get what we pay for.

Many U.S. actors, entertainers and other obscenely rich Americans say "Not in my name" against the war on Iraq, but they pay far more for war than many minimum wage workers who proudly send their soldier sons and daughters to battle. How good is it to proclaim "Not in my name" unless that means "Not with my money?"

Gandhi said, "Be the change you want to see in the world . . . My life is my message."

—Don Schrader, 1810 Silver Ave., SE, Apt.B, Albuquerque, NM 87106. (Excerpts used by permission from *More than a paycheck*, June 2003, and *Mennonite Weekly Review*, November 28, 2005).

APPENDIX RR

Death and Taxes: the Unconscionable Connection

No one argues the certainty of death and taxes. It is the connection between the two that weighs heavily on the consciences of many.

In 2004, 42 cents out of every U.S. income tax dollar paid for the military.[1]

And this year we are asked to pay even more for high-tech weaponry while billions of dollars are cut from social programs. The 2005 U.S. Budget calls for a 7% increase in military spending. By comparison, the increase in domestic, non-homeland security spending is 0.1%.[2] When adjusted for inflation, this negligible increase is actually a net *decrease* in funding for domestic programs.

The Cold War gave rise to the Military Industrial Complex, but the Cold War's end has not brought about a decrease in military spending. Retired Admiral Eugene Carroll, Jr., has assessed the situation in this way: "For 45 years of the Cold War we were in an arms race with the Soviet Union. Now it appears we're in an arms race with ourselves."[3]

The U.S. military budget, $421 billion, exceeds the *combined* military budgets of the 25 next-biggest military spenders in the world![4]

The U.S. military, funded by our tax dollars, does violence on two levels. Obviously, missiles, bombs and guns are designed to destroy. But even if they are never launched, dropped or fired, these weapons do violence by consuming resources that could otherwise have gone to feeding the hungry, housing the homeless, and healing the sick. Many people hold the deep conviction that they cannot pay for this double violence.

U.S. draft law, since World War II, has acknowledged the right to conscientious objection to military participation. Draftees have been given alternatives to serve their country non-militarily. Tax law, however, continues to draft the tax dollars of conscientious objectors (COs) who see no moral difference between killing and paying for someone else to kill.

Despite the lack of legal recognition, COs continue to refuse to pay for war. Some impoverish themselves and their families rather than be legally bound to pay taxes for war. Others risk fines, bank account and property seizures, levies on their wages, and sometimes jail sentences. In 2005, three COs from New Jersey, Joe and Inge Donato and Kevin McKee, were convicted of "felony conspiracy to defraud the United States," the most serious offense in the Internal Revenue Code, for their refusal to pay for war.[5] "We would always have gladly paid our full share of taxes if only the government could assure us that the amount we paid would not go to fund war making," said Joe Donato, who received a 27-month jail term—the harshest sentence for war tax resistance in over 60 years.

McKee and the Donatos, like other COs, are punished for acting on their deepest convictions. In a country founded on ideals of freedom of religion and belief, shouldn't conscientious objectors to military taxation be given a way to pay their taxes without paying for war?

The Religious Freedom Peace Tax Fund Bill, which has been introduced into every Congressional Session since 1972, would provide such an option. This legislation would allow conscientious objection for taxpayers that, on religious or ethical grounds, cannot participate in the funding of war or preparation for war. Taxpayers who now unlawfully withhold the portion of their taxes which supports military spending would be able to pay their full taxes once again, while still giving voice to their conscience.

The Peace Tax Fund Bill is molded in the image of conscientious objection to military service. It would not reduce an individual's tax liability, nor would it directly alter the level of military spending as established by Congress. It would channel the current military portion of a CO's income tax to life-affirming governmental programs.

A Peace Tax Fund would provide an opportunity for as many as 160 million taxpayers to examine their consciences each year on the question of war and taxes. Each year, Congress would report the level of usage of the Peace Tax Fund, providing a measure of the nation's conscience regarding the inhumanity of war.

The Peace Tax Fund Bill, H.R. 2631 in the 109th Congress, has 39 sponsors in the House of Representatives as of the December 2005. At a time when many legislators are caving in to pressure to restrict civil liberties and rely on military might, it is refreshing to see the courage shown by these co-sponsors who believe in the value of conscience, regardless of their own personal beliefs on war. Support for a Peace Tax Fund Bill has expanded beyond just the historic peace churches to many mainline religious bodies who formally endorsed the Peace Tax Fund Bill as a matter of freedom of conscience.

"Both morals and sound policy require that the state should not violate the conscience of the individual," said Chief Justice Harlan Fisk Stone. "All our history gives confirmation to the view that liberty of conscience has a moral and social value which makes it worthy of preservation at the hands of the state . . . . It may well be questioned whether the state which preserves its life by a settled policy of violation of the conscience of the individual will not in fact ultimately lose it by that process."

The movement to respect freedom of conscience continues to grow, even during the current climate of fear and militarism. If this country is to live up to the ideals on which it was founded, conscientious objectors must be given alternative service for their drafted dollars.

[1] Friends Committee on National Legislation
[2] Center on Budget and Policy Priorities "Analysis of the President's Budget" by Richard Kogan and Robert Greenstein, Feb. 5, 2004.
[3] Center for Defense Information "Last of the Big Time Spenders" www.cdi.org.
[4] Friends Committee on National Legislation
[5] *United States v. Joseph Donato et al.*, 04-CR-216 (JBS), District Court of New Jersey.

—Timothy Godshall, Outreach and Development Director, National Campaign for a Peace Tax Fund, 2121 Decatur Place, NW, Washington, D.C. 20008-1923. Used with permission. For more information contact at the address above or at 1-888-PEACE-TAX; Email: info@peacetaxfund.org or visit www. peacetaxfund.org

APPENDIX SS

The Myth of Redemptive Violence

The story that the rulers of domination societies told each other and their subordinates is what we today might call the Myth of Redemptive Violence. It enshrines the belief that violence saves, that war brings peace, that might makes right. It is one of the oldest continuously repeated stories in the world.

The belief that violence "saves" is so successful because it doesn't seem to be mythic in the least. Violence simply appears to be the nature of things. It's what works.

It seems inevitable, the last and, often, the first resort in conflicts. If a god is what you turn to when all else fails, violence certainly functions as a god. What people overlook, then, is the religious character of violence. It demands from its devotees an absolute obedience-unto-death.

This Myth of Redemptive Violence is the real myth of the modern world. It, and not Judaism or Christianity or Islam, is the dominant religion in our society today. I myself first became aware of it, oddly enough, by watching children's cartoon shows. . .

Thankfully, not all children's programs feature explicit violence. But the vast majority perpetuate the mythic pattern of redemptive violence in all its brutality. Examples would include the Teenage Mutant Ninja Turtles, the X-Men, Transformers, the Fantastic Four, Silver Surfer, Ice Man, the Superman family, Captain America, the Lone Ranger and Tonto, Batman and Robin, Roadrunner and Wile E. Coyote, and Tom and Jerry (plus the Power Rangers, where real people act out cartoon characters). . . .

. . .the Myth of Redemptive Violence is the story of the victory of order over chaos by means of violence. It is the ideology of conquest, the original religion of the status quo. The gods favor those who conquer. Conversely, whoever conquers must have the favor of the gods. The common people exist to perpetuate the advantage that the gods have conferred upon the king, the aristocracy, and the priesthood. Religion exists to legitimate power and privilege. Life is combat. Any form of order is preferable to chaos, according to this myth. Ours is neither a perfect nor a perfectible world; it is a theater of perpetual conflict in which the prize goes to the strong. Peace through war; security through strength: these are the core convictions that arise from this ancient historical religion, and they form the solid bedrock on which the Domination System is founded in every society.

The Babylonian myth is far from finished. It is universally present . . .It is the dominant myth in contemporary America. . . .

. . . (We) encounter it in the media, in sports, in nationalism, in militarism, in foreign policy, in televangelism, in the religious right, and in self-styled militia groups. It is celebrated in the Super Bowl, in the Rambo movies, by motorcycle and street gangs, and by the general pursuit of machismo. What appears so innocuous in cartoons is, in fact, the mythic underpinnings of our violent society.

. . .

The myth of redemptive violence is, in short, nationalism become absolute. This myth speaks *for* God; it does not listen for God to speak. It invokes the sovereignty of God as its own; it does not entertain the prophetic possibility of radical judgment by God. It misappropriates the language, symbols, and scriptures of Christianity. It does not seek God in order to change; it embraces God in order to prevent change. Its God is not the impartial ruler of all nations but a tribal god worshiped as an idol. Its metaphor is not the journey but the fortress. Its symbol is not the cross but the crosshairs of a gun. Its offer is not forgiveness but victory. Its good news is not the unconditional love of enemies but their final elimination. Its salvation is not a new heart but a successful foreign policy. It usurps the revelation of God's purpose for humanity in Jesus. It is blasphemous. It is idolatrous.

And it is immensely popular.

I love my country passionately; that is why I want to see it do right. There is a valid place for sensible patriotism. But from a Christian point of view, true patriotism acknowledges God's sovereignty over all the nations, and holds a healthy respect for God's judgments on the pretensions of any power that seeks to impose its will on others. There is a place for a sense of destiny as a nation. But it can be authentically pursued only if we separate ourselves from the legacy of the myth of redemptive violence and struggle to face the evil within ourselves. There is a divine vocation for the United States (and every other nation) to perform in human affairs. But it can perform that task, paradoxically, only by abandoning its messianic pretensions and accepting a more limited role within the family of nations.

This is the context in which the gospel is proclaimed today. And I believe that Jesus' gospel is the most powerful antidote to the myth of redemptive violence that the world has ever known. . . .

. . . Jesus challenged the Domination System of his day right where it affected men and women in the routine of their lives, in the everyday push and pull of relating to the institutions that shaped their times. His words still challenge the manifestations of the Domination System today.

. . .

We must admit our addiction to the Myth of Redemptive Violence—an addiction every bit as tenacious and seductive as bondage to alcohol or drugs. Civilization is hooked on violence. Rational argument, therefore, is not enough to break its grip over us. We need to acknowledge our bondage and turn to a higher power for help in extricating ourselves from our trust in destructive force.

—Walter Wink is professor of Biblical Interpretation at Auburn Theological Seminary in New York City. *The Powers That Be: Theology for a New Millennium* (Minneapolis, MN: Fortress Press, 1998), 42-3, 48-9, 61-3, and 141. Used by permission. A more complete exposition of the Myth of Redemptive Violence is given in his trilogy on "The Powers" (Naming the Powers, Unmasking the Powers, & Engaging the Powers) and in chapter 11 of *The Destructive Power of Religion, Vol. 3* (Westport, Conn. & London: Praeger, 2004) edited by J. Harold Ellens.

APPENDIX TT

War Tax Resistance: A Blessing That Awaits Christians

Imagine the impossible . . .or highly improbable. Imagine that one million middle class Christians in the United States refused to pay taxes for war. Let's not worry for the moment how this came about, except to acknowledge that it grew out of our deep commitment to Christ and the worldwide church.

Furthermore, let's imagine that we cheerfully supported one another in this refusal to pay taxes for war, so that no one need be alone in this act of faith.

What would this do to our churches? What would happen to our witness in the world? How would God change us in the process?

We cannot know with certainty. I am convinced, however, that there are parallels to the blessing that awaited the peace churches when they chose insult and prison rather than military service during World War I. We remember that history and still benefit from that witness.

In this article I imagine what Christians would face if a million of us decided that faithfulness meant the refusal to pay taxes for war.

Simple living, the legal approach

The "more-with-less" approach to life would become the norm in many churches. Vast numbers of Christians would choose legal means of reducing the amount paid in taxes for war. We would reduce our personal incomes and give a

198

higher percentage of our money to churches and charitable organizations in an effort to reduce our tax liability.

There would be an explosion of creativity in this regard. Many Christians would opt for simpler housing and shared living arrangements. We would help young people avoid large long-term mortgages. Living in duplexes or other multiple-unit dwellings would reduce purchase and maintenance costs and save on heat, utilities, appliances, and tools. Shared housing would teach us valuable lessons about community, openness, and hospitality.

More of us, in an effort to reduce expenses, would send our children to public schools and work alongside our neighbors to improve the quality of education for all. Alternately, given our greater interest in tax deductions through charitable contributions, our church schools could be more highly subsidized, less expensive, and thus more accessible to all income groups.

We would purchase fuel-efficient cars, do more walking and biking, and take public transportation.

The same theology, which prevents us from paying taxes for war, would lead us to a fresh examination of our spending priorities. We would grieve the economic injustice and disparity in the world that destroys the hopes of people. Church building and expansion programs would always be reviewed in light of community and world needs. Our churches would struggle deeply with the god of materialism. We would become "economically nonconformed" to this world. It would be usual for people to give 20 to 30 percent of their incomes to the church and charitable organizations to meet basic human needs. It would be routine for a congregation to hire one or two people to work at community needs and concerns.

Refusing to pay taxes for war would expand our understanding of conscientious objection to war. We would understand conscientious objection to include issues related to employment, investments, taxes, lifestyle, and business relationships, in addition to military registration and conscription.

The Religious Freedom Peace Tax Fund Bill would receive all the financial support it needed. Congresspersons would frequently receive mail and visits on the subject. Conscience against war would receive a better hearing in the halls of government.

Tax resistance, the illegal approach

A significant number of Christians would choose the path of tax resistance by withholding the military portion or a symbolic amount of their tax dollars from the Internal Revenue Service (IRS). It would be normal to find a group of families in each congregation who is seeking counsel and support on the issue.

Church-related institutions would honor employee requests not to withhold their income tax dollars. Christian leaders would frequently find themselves in IRS offices and the courts, witnessing to their faith and conscience, and the convictions of their people.

As the public became aware of this expression of Christian faith, some would perceive Christians as a threat. We could become the targets of harassment and community pressure. People would make nasty phone calls and vandalize us as a result of our beliefs, particularly during times of crisis such as the 9/ll or the continuing war on terror.

Some of us could end up in jail, being used as examples to deter others from continuing to practice tax resistance. New Christian fellowships might form in our prisons as a result of the life and witness of tax resisters.

These experiences would make it easier for us to identify with Christians in many parts of the world who sometimes face difficult social or religious pressures in their communities. Our sense of unity with the worldwide church would become stronger.

The perception of Christianity in other countries would slowly begin to change. Rather than being identified with empire and military conquest, Christians would become known as a people of peace. Christians would gain respect both domestically and internationally for practical peacebuilding efforts that champion the cause of the most vulnerable.

We would not have to scratch our heads and wonder how to do peace education with our youth. They would sense that our concern about Christ's way of peace is integral to our life and faith. They would wonder why we are going to court and to jail, and would ask us many difficult questions over dinner and during Sunday school.

Conclusion

War tax resistance is not the only path to the many things mentioned above. Surely we as a church could commit ourselves to simple living and a 10 to 20 percent tithe without the burden (or the blessing) of the war tax issue. Certainly there are other ways to grow in commitment to racial equality or justice for the poor.

In my experience, however, war tax resistance remains one of the most relevant ways to affirm life and peace in a world of war and terror. It has also served as the best discipline for simple living in a culture of materialism and consumption.

Implementing this vision in our churches could lead to conflict and division. It could also lead us to experience anew Christ's reconciling spirit among us. It would not be easy. I am convinced, however, that a great blessing awaits the church when we agree to say yes to Christ's way of peace, by refusing to pay taxes for war. When will it happen? What will become of us if it doesn't?

—Titus Peachey, Director of Peace Education, MCC U.S.; Email: tmp@mcc.org. Used by permission.

APPENDIX UU

Protecting their Territory—A Soldier's Awakening
The US Army kills people for the reason of defending their country.

This is the same thing gangs do. Protect their territory. . . . Growing up in Chicago I was exposed to a lot of violence going on in the city. I was always afraid of being recruited [into a gang]. I didn't realize it until I joined the military and learned exactly what it was all about, that joining the military is like joining a street gang. . . . My conscience would not allow me to join a street gang, so why would I want to be part of an organization that glorifies organized killing?

—Reflections of a CO seeking discharge from the Army; quoted in the *Reporter for Conscience' Sake* (winter, 2001), p. 7. Used by permission of the Center on Conscience & War, 1830 Connecticut Ave., NW, Washington, D.C. 20009. www.CenterOnConscience.org

APPENDIX VV

An Open Letter: Why I Plan to Do Civil Disobedience at SOA
Dear Friends:

I have made conscious decision to become a "prisoner on purpose." By committing civil disobedience this November at the U.S. Army School of the Americas (SOA), I will risk up to 6 months in prison and a $5,000 fine. After attending the SOA Watch vigil numerous times, after organizing groups of people to travel to the vigil at SOA, after numerous letters, calls, and visits to my congress people, after fasting on the Capitol steps, after traveling to El Salvador, after acting as a major support person to an SOA prisoner of conscience in Wichita, I faithfully submit that it is time for me to take this step.

To paraphrase Daniel Berrigan, "You reach a point when you simply cannot not act." The time has come to say "yes" to liberty with a bigger part of my life. I cannot read anymore about the displacement of small farmers in Columbia through deliberate pesticide spraying (under the guise of "war on drugs)." I can no longer hear about good people being massacred for setting up peace settlements. I cannot read anymore about children being chainsawed to death for being "guerrilla sympathizers." I can't in good conscience think about these horrors without vowing to act with a bigger part of my life. This is our tax dollars that supports these acts of terror. If I want the U.S. Government to stop conducting "business as usual" in Latin America," perhaps it's time I stop conducting "business as usual" in my own life.

There is a movie called "In My Country" which depicts the atrocities committed against black persons in South Africa. There's a scene in the movie where a reporter asks a white South Africa woman: "You mean you knew about these atrocities and you didn't do anything?" "We all knew," she said.

Friends, I count myself as one of the ones now who "know." I no longer can stand by paralyzed by the "knowing and not acting." I do not pretend that this terrorist training camp (SOA/WHISC) is some entity totally disconnected from me. I participate in a complicated economic culture that robs others of basic needs and human rights so that I can maintain a higher standard of living. I confess that the fabric of the richest, most consumerist country in the world courses through my veins. SOA helps keep all of this in place.

On the other hand, I see this action as a natural outgrowth of my spirituality. Ched Meyers, in *Binding the Strong Man* contends that Jesus' life was a non-violent campaign of resistance against oppressive powers. Walter Wink says that every action of true nonviolence will have tremendous ripple effects -- effects which we may never be able to fully appreciate. I see this action as a welling over of study, prayer, meditation, mantra, receiving the Eucharist, and communal life.

203

There is also a personal reason I discern this action. Manuel (not real name), a former co-worker and friend previously worked as a union organizer in El Salvador. Manuel told me he was imprisoned in El Salvador for daring to strive for a better life. He and other detainees lived in the stench of a dungeon with a foot of water. He still vividly remembers hearing the screams of agony of fellow detainees being tortured above. He remembers hearing the footsteps of soldiers coming down the steps, all the while wondering if he was next. (There's a real good chance some of these soldiers were trained at SOA). His time did come. The soldiers tortured him horribly and dumped him, emaciated and bleeding, by a river. Thanks to good people of faith from the U.S., Manuel was rescued from sure death and brought to Texas. He eventually landed in Chicago where he and I became friends. I stood next to him one year at SOA as soldiers began walking toward demonstrators waiting at the line of Ft. Benning. Manuel was traumatized all over again by the experience. This was a pivotal moment for me. I am committing to this action for Manuel, and thousands like him who have paid a horrible price for daring to fulfill the yearnings of their human spirit.

Sincerely, Charles Carney

—Charles F. Carney, a citizen of the Midwest, works as a painting contractor and landscaper to support his activism. This includes marches against hunger, promoting alternatives to the death penalty, restoring citizen power over corporations, directing peace and human rights efforts, and offering humanitarian services through the Catholic Worker House in Kansas City, MO. His letter was used by permission. He can be reached by phone (913/ 281-5499) or Email: ccarney_1@juno.com

APPENDIX WW

Looking in the Mirror to See the Face of War

The *Catholic Worker* movement will celebrate its seventieth anniversary in May. Looking back, I am amazed to realize I have been with them for two-thirds of that history. I met Dorothy Day and Ammon Hennacy forty-six years ago when I was twenty. The day we met I went to jail with them to serve thirty days for a Cold War civil defense protest. In the cell that night Ammon said, "Being a pacifist between wars is like being a vegetarian between meals. "He was a pacifist because he wouldn't kill people, and a vegetarian because he didn't want animals killed for him to eat. He had refused to register for the military draft for both World Wars I and II. He had served two years at Atlanta Penitentiary, nine months in solitary confinement, for his World War I resistance. He was talking about the history of peace movements before both wars. There had been mass movements of Americans opposed to U.S. involvement before both wars that collapsed as soon as war was declared. Many of the peace advocates either volunteered for military service, or quietly submitted to military conscription.

Nowadays, we have a different problem: a lot of people are only pacifists during wars, which is like being vegetarians during meals while working at a factory pig farm to earn a living between meals. Contemporary liberals and internationalists don't want to fight in wars themselves, or waste their tax payments on excessive military spending. We march in the streets whenever the government heads into a hot war. When the hot war ends, the marching ends with it, and most of us go on living in the same way we were living before, which is the same way most other Americans live. Mindless economic growth, and defense of our extravagant way of life, have been both reason and rationale for war and empire throughout the history of this republic, from westward expansion to "Manifest Destiny" to the neoimperialism of the last half-century. We live in an economic and political culture that makes imperial power seem necessary and future wars of domination almost inevitable.

I have struggled nonviolently to end six long wars, in six successive decades, from the '50s through the present. We carried on a forty-year struggle to end the Cold War weapons race with the Soviet Union and its allies. Ending the Vietnam War absorbed our energies in the '60s and '70s. In the '80s, there were three long Central American wars, in El Salvador, Nicaragua, and Guatemala. Then, the continuing Gulf War against Iraq, from 1990 through the present. Along the way there were small neoimperial wars that ended quickly enough that we had little chance to get organized to oppose them: Cuba, the Dominican Republic, Grenada, Panama, Kosovo. The war in Colombia is a long one that has not yet reached the level of mass awareness.

I've grown old in these struggles, I'm getting tired, and I keep on asking, "What's going on here?"

And, "Why am I so discouraged about the future of peace?"

After the 9/11 attack I saw a cartoon showing a table with flags for sale, that was crowded with customers, next to a table with mirrors for sale that had no customers. At this moment, we could add a table with anti-war buttons and bumper stickers, with lots of customers, and still no customers for mirrors.

Gandhi taught that the path of nonviolence begins with self- examination and purification of self. We need to look in the mirror first to see the face of war, before we look at the television screen and start fuming about George Bush.

Excessive petroleum use is the greatest source of violence on Earth today. It pollutes the atmosphere and distorts the ecological balance of Earth. Political tensions over oil resource control are at the root of many contemporary wars. U.S. policymakers believe they must project overwhelming military power around the whole world to control oil energy resources.

The Bushes, Bakers, Cheneys, Rumsfelds know how to secure huge quantities of petroleum required for the American way of life, at prices American voters find acceptable. Many of us are appalled when we have to see the bloody details of how they go about it. Many of us might be ready to use less petroleum energy, or pay more for it, rather than control it through weapons and war. However, electoral results tend to indicate that a majority of Americans who shop for oil in the same marketplace with us prefer to deny or ignore the environmental and human costs, or are consciously willing to accept them.

Unless a whole lot of us begin to live in a radically different way between wars, especially by reducing our personal energy consumption, more bloody struggles over control and pricing of petroleum and other world resources are inevitable.

Let's look in the mirror to see how we are living.

Do we live alone, or with one or two others, in large houses, while hundreds of thousands of our fellow citizens are homeless? Do we leave the thermostat at 68 degrees day and night, even when we are all away earning income to pay the bill, or when we are sleeping? Do we leave lights on and appliances running when we are not using them?

Are we driving motor vehicles for thousands of thoughtless miles each year, on every kind of errand or trip that impulse suggests? For instance, would we drive hundreds of miles to Washington or New York for a one-day rally against oil control wars?

Do we own corporate stocks with large appreciation in value, though much of the work that added to their value was done by people in foreign lands and in our own country who were not decently paid for their labor? Could we find alternative investments in affordable housing and in community based economic development that support justice for the poor?

Do we buy lots of unnecessary products, things for transitory or infrequent use, objects for gifts or personal use that may never be used at all? Is one of our biggest headaches how to store them in closets, basements, garages and attics?

Do we pay high prices for produce imported at all seasons, by gasoline powered transport, from thousands of miles away, from Guatemala, Hawaii, Australia? Do we cut half of it away because of imperfections, or throw it into the garbage to be hauled to landfills after it rots in the refrigerator? What about the fertile land in the yards immediately around our houses? Do we plant most of it in grass, and then scalp it to the ground weekly in summer with gasoline-powered mowers and weedeaters? Could we grow our own berries, fruits and vegetables by hand cultivation within fifty feet of our own houses?

Finally, do we pay taxes for war? The military budget of the United States costs an average of about $1500 for every woman, child and man. Add the yearly interest payments for past military expenditures that were financed by borrowing from the wealthy segments of society. About half of all federal income tax revenues are spent on military costs for the current budget, plus interest on past military borrowing and other costs of past wars. George Bush doesn't want our opinions about spending and war. The government doesn't require us to vote, and Bush doesn't even want us to vote in the next election, for he rightly supposes that we would vote against him. The government no longer drafts young men to fight its wars.

There is only one thing our rulers require of us to sustain the execution of their military policies: they demand that we pay federal income taxes.

If I see that those policies are morally wrong, I feel a moral imperative to resist the taxes that pay for them. Over the last forty-five years, I have talked to thousands of people in peace movements about refusing war taxes. They invariably point out that this could be difficult, and even risky. Yes, it could be. I have refused payment of all federal income taxes for forty-three years. Along the way I've encountered occasional employment and property seizure difficulties. I was even one of the few who've gone to jail for it, serving nine months in federal prison during the Vietnam War, because of my role in organizing war tax refusal. But it was well worth it, and I spent all the money I didn't pay on real social needs that I saw.

In the seventy-year history of the *Catholic Worker* movement, we have responded to all of these questions about how to live in peace. We have lived in community and received homeless people into our "houses of hospitality". We have tried to use buses, trains and bicycles more, and to use automobiles less. We've invested our savings in community development loan funds that finance low-income housing and employment opportunities. We wear second-hand clothes and use second-hand appliances, furniture and building materials. We salvage tons of food from dumpsters, groceries and restaurants. We cultivate organic gardens in the country and on vacant lots near our inner city "houses of hospitality". When we earn enough income to be liable for federal income taxes, lots of us refuse to pay them.

From my life experience I have come to believe that we can not have a peaceful relationship with the whole of Earth until a whole lot of Americans learn to live in a new way. I still cry when I read the closing words of Dorothy Day's autobiography, *The Long Loneliness*, written when the movement was only twenty years old:

The most significant thing about *The Catholic Worker* is poverty, some say.

The most significant thing is community, others say. We are not alone any more.

But the final word is love. At times it has been, in the words of Father Zossima, a harsh and dreadful thing, and our very faith in love has been tried through fire.

We cannot love God unless we love each other, and to love we must know each other. We know Him in the breaking of bread, and we are not alone any more. Heaven is a banquet and life is a banquet, too, even with a crust, where there is companionship.

We have all known the long loneliness and we have learned that the only solution is love and that love comes with community.

It all happened while we sat there talking, and it is still going on.

—Karl Meyer is a member of Nashville Greenlands in Nashville, TN, a non-sectarian community affiliated with the *Catholic Worker* movement. This essay, used by permission, was written in February 2003 in response to the impending U.S. invasion of Iraq. Meyer can be reached by telephone (615/322-9523) or via Email: karlmeyerng@hotmail.com.

Information on simple living, hospitality, and urban gardening: www.catholicworker.com

Information and counseling on war tax refusal methods and consequences: National War Tax Resistance Coordinating Committee, www.nwtrcc.org or 1-800-269-7464

APPENDIX XX

Tax Us for Peace, Not War
Citizens and Dwellers in this fair Willamette Valley, of the State of Oregon, of the United States of America . . . HEAR YE! HEAR YE!

We, the noble group of Taxes for Peace Not War, on this 15th day of April, 2005, Tax Day, do hereby present

A PROCLAMATION!

We proclaim that we, good citizens and dwellers in this fair Willamette Valley, are not represented in the taxation laid upon us by our United States Government.

While huge sums are spent to support our crazy wars, our increasing empire,

weapons in space and nuclear weapons,

While over 2 million are incarcerated in our prisons,

Poverty expands!

Homelessness expands!

Schools are increasingly underfunded!

Health care is increasingly limited!

Our forests are being destroyed, our air and waters polluted!

Policies of corporate globalization cause poverty and devastation around the world,

while they benefit the corporate rich,

And the wealthy of our country do not pay their fair share of taxes!

Our nation is becoming bankrupt!

Is this the way we want our Taxes used?

No!

Tax Us for Peace, Not War!

What Do We Want?

End the war and bring our soldiers home!

Dignified lives for our elders, the disabled, the poor!

Excellent education for our children and youth!

Excellent health care for all!

Protection of our threatened forests, air and water!

Excellent public transportation, urban, rural, and national!

Economic policies that benefit populations around the world!

May we of this fair Willamette Valley, and all people around the country and

the world who seek peace, dignity for all, and true security that might come

from policies of love, unite to achieve these goals!

TAX US FOR PEACE, NOT WAR!

—The above proclamation was created by the Eugene, Oregon group of "Taxes for Peace Not War" and used at their 2005 tax day demonstration. It appeared in *More than a paycheck* (June, 2005) published by the National War Tax Resistance Coordinating Committee (NWTRCC), PO Box 150553, Brooklyn, NY 11215. Permission to reprint granted. Tel. (800/ 269-7464).

APPENDIX YY

"There Is A Spirit"

There is a Spirit which I feel that delights to do no evil, nor to revenge any wrong, but delights to endure all things, in hope to enjoy its own in the end. Its hope is to outlive all wrath and contention, and to weary out all exaltation and cruelty, or whatever is of a nature contrary to itself. It sees to the end of all temptations. As it bears no evil in itself, so it conceives none in thoughts to any other. If it be betrayed, it bears it, for its ground and spring is the mercies and forgiveness of God. Its crown is meekness, its life is everlasting love unfeigned; and takes its kingdom with entreaty and not with contention, and keeps it by lowliness of mind. In God alone it can rejoice, though none else regard it, or can own its life. It's conceived in sorrow, and brought forth without any to pity it, nor doth it murmur at grief and oppression. It never rejoiceth but through sufferings: for with the world's joy it is murdered. I found it alone, being forsaken. I have fellowship therein with them who lived in dens and desolate places in the earth, who through death obtained this resurrection and eternal holy life.

—James Nayler, one of the early leaders of the Society of Friends in England, may have written this statement in 1660. Kenneth Boulding believes "it carries a message of peace to a world at war, a clear wind of pure truth amid the fogs of propaganda

and deceit, an intimation of that love which is indeed God."
Boulding built his 26 sonnets on this statement.

APPENDIX ZZ

The Nayler Sonnets
XIII. For its ground and spring is the mercies and forgiveness of God

My Lord, Thou art in every breath I take,
And every bite and sup taste firm of Thee.
With buoyant mercy Thou enfoldest me,
And holdest up my foot each step I make.
Thy touch is all around me when I wake,
Thy sound I hear, and by Thy light I see
The world is fresh with Thy divinity
And all Thy creatures flourish for Thy sake.

For I have looked upon a little child
And seen Forgiveness, and have seen the day
With eastern fire cleanse the foul night away;
So cleansest Thou this House I have defiled.
And if I should be merciful, I know
It is Thy mercy, Lord, in overflow.

XV. Its life is everlasting love unfeigned

Caught in a mirrored maze of bright deceit,
Peopled with images, that but reflect
The groping movements of the intellect,
Till bounds are smudged where fact and shadow meet,
The mind is lost, until with quickened beat
Love scents a wind, blowing from God, unchecked,
And senses, deeper laid than sight, direct
To the free air our once-bewildered feet.

But love must be made pure to be our guide;
Not trader's love, that seeks more in return,
But love that with clear, slender flame will burn
Though it be spent for nought, spurned, crucified,
Until to one vast song our spirit lifts:
To love for Love alone, not for His gifts.

—Kenneth E. Boulding, *There is a Spirit: The Nayler Sonnets*. Used courtesy of the Fellowship of Reconciliation (www.forusa.org).

Donald D. Kaufman was born in 1933 and nurtured in the farming community of southeastern South Dakota. As a generalist he has done administrative work in Indonesia, pastoral ministry in the Midwest, managed public housing in Kansas, and provided resident care for clients with disabilities. He also has assisted families with the construction of Habitat for Humanity houses and visited prison inmates to promote restorative justice.

As an elementary student during World War II he experienced social pressure to support scrap metal drives, to cooperate in "blackouts," and to purchase war bonds. The formative influence of his parents coupled with the Anabaptist and Peacemaker movements led him to explore the ethics of how one ought to live in a world of cruel realities—the "principalities and powers" under which every citizen lives.

He received his MDiv degree from the Associated Mennonite Biblical Seminary (Elkhart, Ind.) in 1969. His AA and BA degrees came through Freeman Jr. College (1953) and Bethel College (1955) respectively. Bethany Theological Seminary granted his BDiv degree in 1958. He benefited from four quarters of Clinical Pastoral Education under the supervision of Robert Carlson. Kaufman's writings have appeared in periodicals and study papers. He is the author of two books on the complicity of paying military taxes. His first book, What Belongs to Caesar?, was published by Herald Press (1969) and has since been reprinted by Wipf and Stock Publishers.

Donald is married to Eleanor Gross Wismer of Hilltown, Pennslyvania. They are the parents of three adult children: Kendra, Galen, and Nathan. For Kaufman life is both miracle and mystery. The childhood patterns of wondering about life never cease. Neither does the adventure. There are tears of both grief and laughter. Life is good because others listen and care. He is sustained by an amazingly large community of love. The Gospel offers him a love that transcends sentimentality, a faith that can live with doubt, and a hope that is able to confront despair. These values give meaning and purpose to his life.